The Great Clay Adventure

The Great Clay Adventure

Creative Handbuilding for Young Artists

Ellen Kong

Davis Publications, Inc.
Worcester, Massachusetts

Printed in Italy
Library of Congress Number: 98-87487

ISBN 10: 0-87192-389-0
ISBN 13: 978-0-87192-389-9
10 9 8 7 6 5 4

Publisher: Wyatt Wade

Editorial Director: Claire Mowbray Golding

Production Editors: Laura Marshall Alavosus, Nancy Burnett

Assistant Editor: Mary Ellen Wilson

Manufacturing Coordinator: Jenna Sturgis

Copyeditor: Lauren Kaufman

Design: Janis Owens

Contents

Part Five
Sound in Clay

Part Six
Large Group Projects

Acknowledgments

To my husband, David, whose support and understanding make all things possible.

The talent, energy, and ebullience of my Durham Academy students colors the pages of this book. Our creating and exploring together has filled many days with mutual delight and precious joy.

I sincerely thank Donald North, former Headmaster of Durham Academy, for his thoughtful suggestions during the early stages of this book. Jim Speir, Dean of Faculty at Durham Academy, provided valuable support. The dear friendship and boundless enthusiasm of my colleagues Mary North and Yolanda Litton were irreplaceable during this project.

I extend profound gratitude to the editors at Davis Publications, particularly Claire Golding, Helen Ronan, Nancy Burnett, and Laura Alavosus, who made the gestation and delivery of this book a fun and exciting endeavor.

Deepest appreciation goes to my warm and sustaining family, who contributed the very best of their individual talents. My wonderful daughter, Stephanie, provided continual e-mail inspirations from across the Atlantic. My son, David, Jr., tirelessly reviewed the entire manuscript between pages to the ER and ICU. My husband, David, Sr., expertly photographed all of the claywork with inimitable patience and attention to detail.

Finally, I salute the teachers, parents, and mentors who have devoted their lives to shaping young children as masterfully as potters mold clay.

Introduction

Art education is a continuous process, stimulating growth in sensory awareness and visual recall. Acquiring art skills helps students interpret their perceptions and translate their impressions into creative self-expression. Students make original artwork by intentionally choosing lines, shapes, colors, forms, space, and textures. They learn to use the principles of art—balance, variety, harmony, emphasis, proportion, movement, rhythm, and unity—as guidelines to combine visual elements.

In an effective art curriculum, students learn sequentially. They gain valuable art concepts when they advance from basic knowledge to abstract critical thinking. *The Great Clay Adventure* provides core ideas and field-tested examples for a sequential art curriculum. The clay projects start with simple concepts, skills, and techniques, first individually and then combined. Each successive lesson builds upon the previous ones. The instructional strategies use a variety of teaching techniques for presenting art concepts and provide practice activities for sharpening art skills.

The activities in this book are designed to focus elementary and middle school students' attention on dynamic, interactive, clay handbuilding techniques. Interdisciplinary curricular designs bridge art and core curricula and foster cooperative learning. Several lesson plans include multicultural approaches to promote appreciation of cultural diversity and critical thinking skills.

The evaluation criteria supplied for each lesson are checkpoints to assess students' learning. They are the expected achievements of each activity, and should provide some assurance that students are learning what the lesson intends to teach. Assessment of learning also helps students recognize their strengths and areas that need work. Advanced or artistically gifted students can further develop their potential through the enrichment activities listed at the end of the lessons.

Part One

First Forays with Clay

Fundamentals

Knee and Elbow Pots

Pinch Pots

Coil Beads

1

Fundamentals

Objectives

- Name and describe the four elements of pottery making.
- Identify the material properties of clay.
- Recognize the different appearances of manipulated clay.
- Develop confidence and essential motor skills.

A potter looks through the peephole during Raku firing. When the glaze surface shines like melting ice, the work will be removed from the kiln and smoked in a metal container filled with sawdust, pine needles, shavings, or shredded newspaper.

Earth, air, water, and fire comprise the essential elements of pottery making. Clay emerges from the earth, dries when exposed to air, and softens when blended with the right amount of water. When fired to maturity, clay strengthens greatly through the fusion of its component particles. Once hardened by the kiln, it never returns to its plastic stage.

Clay becomes very friendly after its properties and limitations are understood. During the past two billion years, the ceaseless motion of mountain upheavals, wind, ice, and rain has ground rock into grains of clay. Clay is weathered, decomposed granite that consists mainly of alumina and silica. Students often confuse clay with garden soil, which contains clay, sand, and humus. To teach students more about the origins of clay, look for age-appropriate geology or earth sciences books at your local library.

Characteristics of Clay:
Hardness, Porosity, Color, Plasticity, and Shrinkage

Finished clayworks can be classified into three distinct groups according to fired density: earthenware, stoneware, and porcelain. These terms also indicate other characteristics such as color, workability, and tactile quality. In general, earthenware clay is a low-temperature (about 1700–2100° F) firing clay. The fired piece is not waterproof. Stoneware clay is a medium to high-temperature (about 2100–2350° F) firing clay. The appearance of its dense surface without a glaze makes it popular with potters. The fired stoneware is waterproof. Porcelain is a high-temperature (above 2300° F) firing clay. Fired porcelain is hard, dense, and translucent when thin.

While some potters mine clay for their creations, digging and preparing clay is usually not economical. A completely satisfactory clay body seldom occurs in nature, and the refining processes are laborious. Environmental health and safety concerns require careful consideration. Commercial moist clay is well blended, de-aired, and consistent in quality. It is best stored in its original plastic bag inside the manufacturer's cardboard box. Air will inevitably work its way into the clay, even through the unopened cardboard box. An airtight, heavy-duty polyethylene storage cart will keep the clay moist for months.

Clay colors include white, buff, gray, red, brown, and black. The color of the clay may change upon firing. A few simple tests prior to use will familiarize you with a new clay. Test tiles demonstrating the clay in different stages are valuable teaching tools.

Test tiles: terra cotta clay (bottom row) and white earthenware clay (top row). Left to right: leather-hard tiles, bone-dry tiles, bisques, glazed tiles before firing, glazed tiles fired to maturity.

Plasticity is essential to handbuilding. To test plasticity, loop a pencil-size coil of clay around your finger. If the coil cracks a lot, it probably will not work well with students. Aging improves the workability and plasticity of clay bodies, as water slowly penetrates and binds clay particles together. Ancient Chinese potters stored clay for years, aging it for the next generation. The simplest way to improve the plasticity of clay bodies is to leave some old clay in the containers to accelerate bacterial growth. Bacterial gel promotes elasticity in clay.

Wedging or kneading the clay improves workability. Wedging helps to evenly distribute the moisture in clay and drive out trapped air. All clay contains air. If air bubbles remain in the clay, they will expand and burst during firing. Wedging is a ritual that prepares the potter to work with clay. Wedging instills discipline, just as ink grinding prepares Chinese artists for painting or calligraphy. Wedging clay with rocking and kneading motions requires physical strength. The simplest method is to vigorously throw the lump of clay on the workboard ten to fifteen times. This will expel the air and solidify the clay.

A clay body shrinks as it dries in the air and during firings. The amount of **shrinkage** depends on the clay formula (the recipe) and the temperature to which it is fired. Usually, more plastic clays shrink the most. It is easy to measure shrinkage. First, roll out the clay slab, and cut or mark it to a measure. Measure again when the slab is bone-dry. Take a final measurement after the clay slab has been fired to maturity.

Basic Procedures: Drying and Firing

To prevent warping and cracking, air dry all projects evenly, slowly, and thoroughly. Turn the clayworks over from time to time, or dry them on a rack that allows air to circulate. Keep them away from sun and drafts. It may be necessary to cover a newly formed, moist claywork with a thin plastic sheet to retard its drying. Protect thinner sections or small appendages with plastic to equalize the drying rate of the entire piece.

The clay will toughen as moisture slowly evaporates from the clay. The outer surface of the clay feels cool, but the interior is still damp. At this stage, the clay is called **leather hard**. When clay contains about two percent moisture at room temperature, it is warmer and lighter in weight. At this stage, it is considered **bone-dry**. Objects that are bone-dry are fragile and usually have a chalky appearance. Clay work must never be set into a kiln before it is bone-dry.

Firing is a process that transforms clay from a soft and pliable lump to a hard and permanent object. This process continues to seem magical no matter how many years one works with clay. **Greenware** is pottery that has not been fired. Greenware that has undergone a low-temperature (1600–1850° F) firing prior to glazing is called **bisque.**

To discover the art of clay, you need to understand firing techniques. Electric kilns are most compatible with the demands of students' clay programs. They are particularly suitable for low-fire work. New electronic controllers can automatically monitor firing. As a result, modern electric kilns are simple to operate and produce highly reproducible results. Potters who use the electric kiln should use clay bodies and glazes formulated for oxidation firing.

Kilns come in all shapes and sizes. Some heavy-duty kilns are designed for schools and studios. There is also a wide variety of kilns that are made for home use. Furthermore, many neighborhood pottery studios or craft centers offer kiln firing services at reasonable prices. The best guide to successful firing is your kiln manual, which tells how to prepare the kiln for firing and recommends firing procedures. In general, the electric kiln does not require a great deal of maintenance. However, the elements become fragile after the kiln has been used a few times. It is important not to knock them accidentally with clayworks when loading or unloading the kiln.

When loading the kiln, leave about an inch between the elements and the clayworks. Greenwares may touch each other. Stack large and heavy pieces on the bottom of the kiln. Place tall and light pieces on the upper levels. Leave enough space between clay pieces for the warm air to circulate. For glaze firing, you need to be even more careful. Make sure there is not even a speck of glaze on the bottom of your work.

A In a bisque firing, pots can be stacked on top of one another, foot-to-foot, rim-to-rim, or one inside another.

B In a glaze firing, pieces cannot touch one another.

A

B

Leave at least ¾" (2 cm) between glazed pieces.

During the glaze firing process, when glazes reach their melting point, they boil, bubble, and melt. If two pieces of glazed work are touching, they will stick together. If there is glaze left on the bottom of the claywork, the piece will stick to the kiln shelf, and you will need a hammer and chisel to get it off. When the kiln is carefully packed, set the kiln control at low and start the firing cycle according to your kiln manual. The golden rule of firing is *slowly to heat and slowly to cool.* By keeping a log of all firings, you will gather valuable information about using your kiln.

For those without a kiln or with limited access to one, there are many kinds of oven-fired and self-hardening clays available through art suppliers. Oven-fired clay is a clay body with an additive enabling maturation at 350° F in about an hour. These temperatures are easily attained in an ordinary kitchen oven. Do not attempt to fire clay in a microwave oven. Oven-fired clay comes in white, buff, brown, and terra cotta. Oven-fired clay permits ideal introductory clay experiences for both students and adults. However, it is very important to follow the manufacturer's instructions on baking temperatures and procedures.

Specially formulated, self-hardening clays are also available. Self-hardening clay has been mixed with an additive to produce durability without firing. It can be modeled, sculpted, thrown on a potter's wheel, or used for handbuilding projects. By using self-hardening clay, students can experience many different kinds of modeling. When dry, modeled objects are hard and durable but not waterproof. These objects may be decorated with acrylics or other finishes.

Polymer clay is a synthetic material. This nontoxic, oven-baked clay has become popular in recent years. It has the advantage of not requiring a kiln, but it is much more expensive than natural clay.

When students are given a lump of clay, their first reaction is to move it around in their hands, squeezing it and changing its shape. By poking, pulling, rolling, and pinching, students create odd shapes. From a small ball of moist clay, a dinosaur, bird, or pleasing abstract form may emerge. Tall mountain ranges, vast canyons, rolling ridges, winding tunnels, secret caves, raging volcanoes, and active seas are created by poking, pulling, pinching, and squeezing. The students' sense of discovery, overwhelming energy, and enthusiasm transform initial muddy handshakes into warm earthy embraces.

Evaluation Criteria

- Do students understand the relationship among the essential elements of pottery making?
- Can students identify clay components that have been poked, pulled, pinched, or squeezed?

Above:
Native American potters fire pots in a clearing behind their houses. The firing area must be level and free of trees and bushes.

Above, right:
Acoma potters load pots and prepare for firing. Low humidity and no wind is essential.

Right:
In the Asian "hill kiln," the fire is at the lower end of a long tube. Heat rises to the high end of the chamber, and escapes through the top flue. This is an *anagama*. Courtesy Ursula Goebels-Ellis.

Extensions

Interdisciplinary and Multicultural Link

■ **Science:** Read earth science books to discover how clay is made.

Enrichment Tips

■ Discuss ethnic firing methods. Japanese raku firing is unusual and dramatic. The firing speed, flame, and smoke all contribute to unpredictable results. Native American potters usually fire their pots on metal racks supported by tin cans behind their houses. Good weather and plenty of cow dung are all they need.

■ Show pictures of the Asian "hill kiln," the multiple chambers *noborigama* or *anagama*. The total firing cycle of these gigantic kilns will last for two to three weeks.

2

Knee and Elbow Pots

Objectives

- Develop a rudimentary understanding of the pottery-making process.

Students quickly tire of merely manipulating clay. They soon want to see their creations fired, glazed, and finished. Every student possesses creative and artistic abilities. Providing students with suitable learning materials fosters intellectual growth. Choosing an appropriate clay body ensures an enjoyable learning experience.

There are several factors to consider when choosing a clay body:

1. Handbuilding clay should be plastic and quite strong. If the clay contains **grog** (ground, fired clay) to increase strength, it should be moderate; otherwise, students' hands will suffer.
2. Light-colored clay will not stain clothing. Underglazes and glazes often look best when applied over light-clay body.
3. The clay body and glaze must be compatible in firing temperature. If the clay body matures at a lower temperature than the applied glaze, the claywork may deform when the glaze reaches its maturity.
4. Always choose nontoxic materials. Read and heed the manufacturer's instructions.

A knee pot shows the unique textures of knee and finger marks. There is often a natural flowing waviness at the rim of a knee pot.

Getting Started

Before students begin clay projects, make sure the room, tools, and furnishings are adequately protected from clay dust and particles. Proper use of an air cleaning system is strongly recommended. If you don't have a ventilation system, place a three-speed exhaust fan in an open window. To provide proper ventilation, be sure to open a window or door opposite the exhaust fan. Clean all exposed surfaces with damp sponges at the end of each working day to reduce airborne dust.

Each student needs a good work surface, such as stretched canvas stapled to an 18" (46 cm) square plywood board or wallboard. Students can turn the board to manipulate their projects from all sides, and they may use it to carry finished work to the drying rack without unnecessary handling. Wrap unfinished claywork in airtight plastic to retain moisture throughout the working stage. Dry cleaning bags work well.

Knee and elbow pots introduce young students to the essentials of the clay work process. The clay surface records both the student's individuality and the learning experience.

To create a good work surface, stretch a 22 x 22" canvas and staple it to an 18"-square, 1"-thick plywood board or wallboard.

Materials

For each student

- Clay (about ¾ pound), hands, elbows, and knees are the only tools and materials required for these simple pots.

Clay Alternatives

- Earthenware clay
- Stoneware clay
- Porcelain
- Raku clay
- Oven-fired clay
- Self-hardening clay

Directions

3

1. Place a ball of soft, well-wedged clay the size of an orange on the workboard.
2. Gently pat the clay ball, flattening it slightly until it resembles a jelly-filled donut.
3. Grab the clay donut, keeping the fingers spread widely. **(A)**
4. Lift the clay donut, and press it firmly against one bent knee. Make sure that both hand and knee are imprinted on the clay surface before letting go. The kneecap forms the inside shape of the pot, while the fingers create a scalloped texture on the outside walls. **(B)**
5. To make an elbow pot, press the clay donut against the bent elbow instead of the knee. **(C)**
6. Place pots on a flat surface and let them dry slowly before firing.

A The back of a knee pot shows widespread finger marks. These shell-like textures act like "feet" to elevate the pot. Mark Chandler, age 8.

B Mark flattened a soft clay ball before making a knee pot over his bent knee.

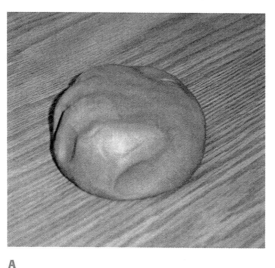

A

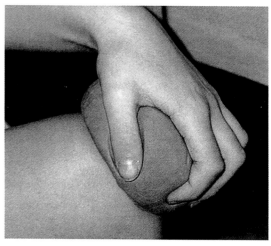

B

C Mark makes an elbow pot by pushing his elbow against the clay while pressing the clay with his hand.

C

Evaluation Criteria

- Do students understand why clay must be well wedged before modeling?
- Have students made knee pots or elbow pots?
- Do students understand the importance of eliminating clay dust?

Extensions

Interdisciplinary and Multicultural Link

- **Science:** Discover the individuality and commonality of body parts, such as knees and elbows.

Enrichment Tips

- Demonstrate the traditional wedging techniques:
  1. Dog's Head Wedging: Wedge a small lump of clay—the size of a grapefruit—with both hands and even pressure. The wedged lump of clay resembles a dog's head.
  2. Spiral Wedging: Wedge a large lump of clay—larger than a grapefruit—with both hands, but press one hand harder than the other. The wedged lump of clay is spiral.

Applying the Fundamentals

Pinch Pots

Objectives

- Make a pinch pot.
- Recognize the simplicity, evenness, and symmetric qualities of pinch pots.

The pinch method is an easy way to make a pot from a ball of clay. However, to fashion a round pinch pot with a thin wall and even rim requires a delicate touch and a certain amount of practice. Pinching is an excellent way to gain technical skills and to develop sensitivity to shape, form, and tactile qualities.

Children often get excited when first introduced to clay. Their hands may pinch too quickly. Remind them to work slowly, steadily, and rhythmically. The tennis ball method described in this chapter is an excellent way to help young children create pinch pots with a rhythmic movement. The tennis ball also helps to re-center the pot during modeling. It is particularly helpful when making sphere and egg shapes from two pots of identical diameter.

Beginners often make lopsided, wobbly pinch pots. However, pinch pots do not have to stand alone. They can be joined side by side to create a new clustered form that takes on a life of its own. Wavy rims can be trimmed with a pair of scissors.

Notice the thin, even walls of this simple, round pinch pot.

Materials

For each student
- [ ] Clay (¾ pound), well-wedged and about the size of an orange
- [ ] Tennis ball
- [ ] An old sock
- [ ] Workboard

Clay Alternatives
- [ ] Earthenware clay
- [ ] Stoneware clay
- [ ] Porcelain
- [ ] Raku clay
- [ ] Oven-fired clay
- [ ] Self-hardening clay

Directions

1. Place the moist clay on the work-board, and roll it into a round ball.
2. Stand up. Look down directly on the clay ball. Imagine it is an orange.
3. Use an index finger to make a dent where the imaginary orange stem would be. **(A)**
4. Remove your index finger from the dent.
5. Push your thumb downwards at the dent. Expand the dent to form a hole that extends to ½" (1 cm) of the bottom.
6. Hold the clay ball with one hand. Place the thumb of the other hand inside the hole, and the remaining fingers around the sides of the clay ball. Pinch the clay between your thumb and fingers. Continue pinching while rotating the pot slowly with the pinching hand. **(B)**
7. Widen the hole by placing both thumbs inside the pot and all fingers around the outside. Pinch with both hands. Rotate the pot slowly between pinches to make the pot uniform in thickness. **(C)**

A Carver Carr, age 9, marks the center of the clay ball with her index finger.

A

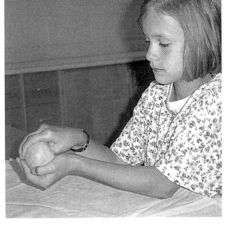

B

B Carver presses her thumb into the ball of clay and pinches the clay between her thumb and fingers.

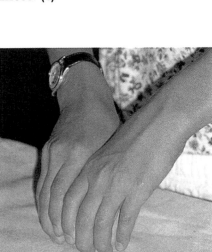

C

C Next she pinches with both hands while rotating the pot slowly between pinches. The thickness of the pot can be felt between fingers and thumb.

8. Continue pinching until the mouth of the pot has widened to the size of a tennis ball.
9. Place the tennis ball inside the sock. Next, invert the pot and place it over the stockinged tennis ball.
10. Gently pat the bottom of the pot. Turn the pot around slowly after two or three pats with your palm. Be sure to have a rhythmic relationship between your patting hand and the rotating ball. **(D)**
11. Don't leave too much clay at the bottom or make the mouth too thin.
12. After the shape is completed, remove the tennis ball. Allow the pot to dry by resting it on its rim. This will help flatten the rim.

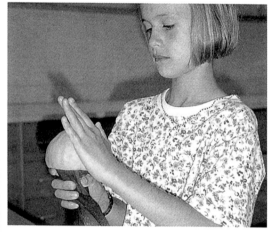

D

D Carver thins out the pinch pot, keeping a rhythmic relationship between her patting hand and the rotating ball.

Seeing is Believing

One picture is better than a thousand words. Try using a transparent hosiery container instead of clay to clarify the process for children. By demonstrating the hand and finger positions with a transparent "pot," children can see the interior and exterior of the pinch pot at the same time.

Carver demonstrates the hand and finger positions with a transparent "pot."

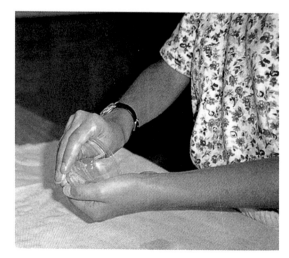

Evaluation Criteria

- Have students modeled pinch pots?
- Are the pots round and even in thickness?
- Are their pots lightweight?

Extensions

Multicultural and Interdisciplinary Links

- **Art:** Learn about Japanese Sumi-e painting.
- **Language Arts:** Examine the role of tea in literature through reading books such as *Alice's Adventures in Wonderland*, *The Tale of Peter Rabbit*, and *Johnny Tremain*.
- **Social Studies:** Research the role of tea and tea sets in history. Learn about British customs, Russian traditions, Asian rituals, the role of tea in the American Revolution and in the development of eighteenth-century commerce.

Enrichment Tips

- Show children pictures of Japanese teacups. Ask them to describe what they see.
- Encourage children to discuss what they think of *simplicity* and *tranquility* in art forms.
- Pass around commercial porcelain teacups, and let children "pinch" and "stroke" them with their eyes closed to feel the evenness and roundness.

4

Adding on New Experiences

Coil Beads

Objectives

- **Understand the basic techniques of rolling clay coils.**
- **Use the coil-forming technique to model beads.**

This book is based on the principle of sequential learning. Like any subject area, art should be taught in a systematic, coherent, and meaningful fashion. Students become disinterested and bored when they are denied new art skills and fresh techniques to satisfy their creative needs. Many clay experiences "build" on one another. Therefore, before we engage in coil projects, we must learn how to make basic coils. Rolling an even coil is an important skill. Once students have mastered this technique, they can progress to a series of coil-building adventures.

These beads are made from coils and decorated with freehand drawings and *mishima* designs which are made by applying slip to textured clay and then scraping away the slip after the clay dries.

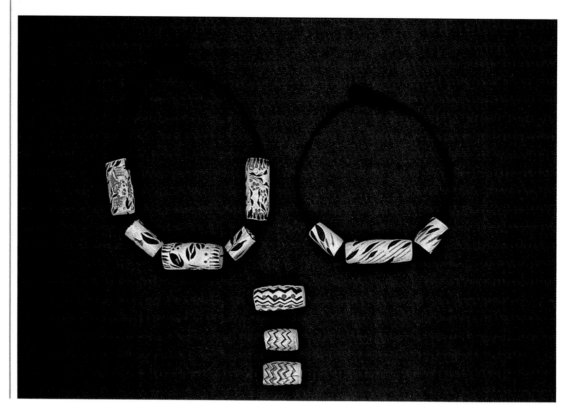

Making Basic Coils

For each student	**Clay Alternatives**
☐ Clay, well-wedged and soft, the size of a stick of butter	☐ Earthenware clay
	☐ Stoneware clay
☐ Workboard	☐ Porcelain
	☐ Raku clay
For each group	☐ Oven-fired clay
☐ Cutting wire	☐ Self-hardening clay
☐ Spray bottle, filled with water (empty and well-washed plastic household sprayer)	☐ Polymer clay

Directions

1. With the cutting wire, cut a piece of clay the size of a stick of butter.
2. Wrap your fingers around the clay stick and squeeze it into a stubby rope. **(A)**
3. Place the clay rope on the workboard. Keep the work surface damp by misting it with water.
4. Place your fingers outstretched at the center of the coil. Exert a steady pressure downward and roll the coil back and forth against your palms.

While rolling, move the palms apart from the middle of the coil to gradually lengthen and thin it. **(B)**

5. Many beginners roll "square" coils. To avoid this, try rolling while standing and leaning over the table slightly. Roll long, even strokes with elbows kept close to the body. If the clay still flattens on two sides, pat it back into shape and continue rolling.

To make clay coils by hand, first squeeze the clay stick into a stubby rope, then roll it into a coil on a flat surface.

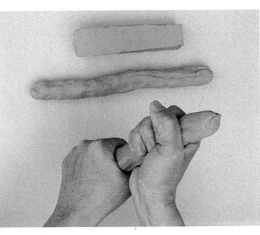

A

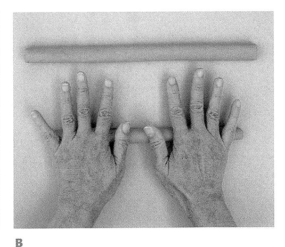

B

Making Coil Beads

Students love creating wearable art. Clay beads are simple and fun to make. Every bead is unique and personal. You can use any clay body: high-firing clay, low-firing clay, oven-fired clay, self-hardening clay, or polymer clay. All of them have their place in bead making.

Older students or adults who are interested in making miniatures, jewelry, or ornaments but don't have access to a kiln should consider using polymer clay. Follow the basic directions and create your own variations.

Materials

For each student
- [ ] Clay (¹⁄₁₆ pound) about the size of a golf ball, well wedged and soft
- [ ] Workboard

For each table
- [ ] Cutting wire
- [ ] Fettling knife
- [ ] An assortment of found objects that make interesting textures

(seashells, magic marker caps, hair rollers, earrings, pins, plastic utensils, nails, cord, lollipop sticks, macaroni, wheels from toy vehicles, building blocks, paper clips, nut shells, craft sticks, tree bark, and bottle caps)
- [ ] Dry alphabet pasta glued on a short skewer to make miniature alphabet stamps.

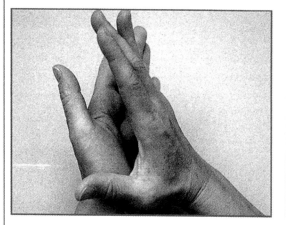

To make a basic round bead, begin by rolling a small bit of clay into a ball.

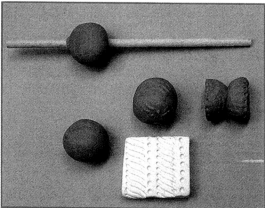

To make a textured bead, roll a round bead over a clay stamp or any interesting textured object. Consider cutting the round textured clay bead in half and joining the two parts back to back to create a new bead form.

Directions

1. From a lump of wedged clay, cut off a piece the size of a golf ball. Squeeze it into a stubby rope.
2. Place the short clay rope on the workboard, and roll it into a thin coil about ½" (1 cm) in diameter.
3. Slice the coil into beads of desirable length (1½–2"/4–5 cm are good sizes for young students).
4. Designs may be pressed onto the bead at this stage. Students may enjoy pressing their names or initials with the miniature alphabet stamps. It is also helpful for labeling their work.

5. Allow the beads to dry until leather hard.
6. Pierce a hole through the center of each bead with a long nail, a bamboo skewer, a knitting needle, or a piece of dry spaghetti. A small hole-cutter is a handy tool for cutting clean holes.
7. Make sure the hole is large enough for stringing. Remember some shrinkage will occur during firing.
8. Allow the beads to dry slowly.
9. Fire to maturity.

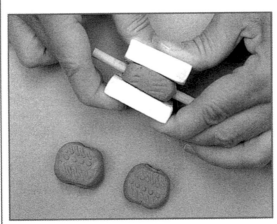

To make a textured flat bead, first make a round bead. Do not remove the dowel after poking the bead hole. Sandwich the clay bead between two clay stamps and squeeze firmly. Then remove the dowel.

To make a tube bead, press a small clay ball into a disk. After adding texture to the disk, bend the disk around your finger and pinch the back together.

These miniature alphabet stamps are made of dry pastas.

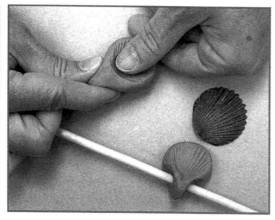

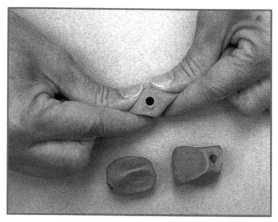

To make this decorative bead, pinch one end of a clay ball with your fingers and press the opposite end with your thumb.

Pinch opposite sides of the clay ball at the same time to make beads with organic shapes.

Evaluation Criteria

■ Do students understand the basic techniques of rolling coils?
■ Did students use proper coil-forming skills when making clay beads?

Extensions

Interdisciplinary and Multicultural Links

■ **Social Studies:** Explore Native American beadwork. Identify the uses of beads. Northeastern tribes used clamshell beads *(wampum)* as money while Plains Indians wove beads on looms.
■ **Mathematics:** Explore the history and development of the abacus.

Enrichment Tips

■ To make textured beads, roll a large bead with soft clay. Pierce a hole through the moist clay bead. Thread the bead with the piercing tool. Grasp the ends of the piercing tool, and roll the bead on textured objects. More rolling lengthens the bead and enlarges the hole.
■ To make uniform-sized beads quickly, use a wire egg cutter or cheese cutter to slice the coil.

Part Two

Pinch and Coil Combinations

Turtles

Coil Animals

Pinch Pot Baskets

Animal Pitchers
and Fountains

Owls

5

Turtles

Objectives

- Use slip and scoring techniques to join two clay surfaces.
- Combine pinch and coil techniques.

Students enjoy a new art process more fully when they become deeply involved with the subject or the techniques. Storytelling, especially fairy tales with multilayered meanings or open-ended conclusions, sparks students' imagination. Students love to act out the stories and make up their own endings. They eagerly draw and model the characters. You will be amazed at what different students perceive in their mind's eye.

Several books, including *The Great Turtle Drive* by Steve Sanfield, *Franklin's Bad Day* by Paulette Bourgeois, and *Coyote and Little Turtle*, based on a story by Herschel Talashoema, may stimulate students' interest in hatching clay tortoises.

Before students venture further into handbuilding techniques, add **slip** and **score** to their vocabulary. Slip is clay mixed with water to a heavy cream consistency. It acts as glue between pieces of clay. Slip made from dried clay sticks better than slip made from wet clay. To create an optimum bond, both surfaces must be scored (scratched) with a pin tool or knife in a cross-hatched pattern. Now, if you can remember how to pinch a pot and roll a few coils, you are ready to hatch a turtle from a lump of clay!

This turtle is a pinch pot and coil combination by Ken Greenleaf, age 11. Ken created the texture on the turtle shell with the cap of a magic marker.

Materials

For each student
- [ ] Clay (1–1¼ pound)
- [ ] Slip
- [ ] Workboard
- [ ] Pin tool
- [ ] Tennis ball
- [ ] An old sock
- [ ] Found object to make patterns on turtle shell

Clay Alternatives
- [ ] Earthenware clay
- [ ] Stoneware clay
- [ ] Porcelain
- [ ] Raku clay
- [ ] Oven-fired clay
- [ ] Self-hardening clay
- [ ] Polymer clay

Directions

1. Use the clay, tennis ball, and sock to make a pinch pot with a thick rim (see Chapter 3). This will become the turtle's shell.
2. With the tennis ball inside the clay pot for support, use found objects to texture the turtle shell.
3. Let the turtle shell rest on its rim.
4. Roll a long coil about ¾" (2 cm) in diameter. Cut five sections, each about 2½" (6 cm) long. From the coil sections, model four legs and a head.
5. Or use the pin tool to slice the head for a smiling whimsical turtle. **(A and B)**
6. Make a tiny pointed tail by rolling only one end of a thin coil.
7. Score the **inside** of the pinch pot where the legs, head, and tail will be attached.
8. Apply slip to the scored areas inside the pinch pot.
9. Score and apply slip to the legs, head, and tail surfaces to be joined to the turtle shell.
10. Join the legs, head, and tail to the turtle shell. The turtle now looks like an upside down chair. **(C)**
11. Bend legs, head, and tail outward, and set the turtle right side up to dry. **(D)**
12. Bisque-fire to maturity when the clay turtles are bone-dry.

To ensure that the legs and head do not separate from the turtle shell, join all coils with slip and weld them carefully to the pinch pot.

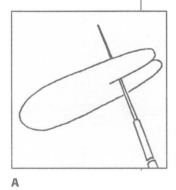

A

B

C

D

Poem illustration,
Emerich Gutter, age 9.
Photograph by Mary
McLean.

Leatherback

Black as midnight
Spotted as stars
Dives the deepest
Huge, bulk, humongous,
mammoth,
Endanger, biggest, dark,
But still a gentle giant.
An ancient nomad.

**Emerich Gutter,
third grade**

Evaluation Criteria

⚖️

■ Can students identify slip components?
■ Can students explain and demonstrate how slip is used?
■ Do students know how to achieve an optimum bond between clay surfaces?
■ Do students skillfully use pinch and coil methods?

Extensions

👁

Interdisciplinary and Multicultural Links

■ **Science:** Study sea turtle habitats and behavior, adaptations to aquatic life, reasons for conservation and protection of threatened species.
■ **Language Arts:** Encourage students to write poems about life as a sea turtle.
■ **Art:** Invite interested students to make illustrations to accompany their sea turtle poems.
■ **Social Studies:** Investigate ethnic attitudes toward turtles by reading myths and legends from around the world.

Enrichment Tips

■ By using pinch and coil methods, students can make spiders and octopuses.
■ Students may make snails by making pinch pots for the shells, emphasizing the spiral shell patterns with small coils and using larger coils for the bodies.

6

Advanced Creatures

Coil Animals

Students enjoy freestanding sculptures. They find animals delightful subjects to model, especially after a trip to the zoo, fair, circus, or science museum. Sometimes it is difficult to remember the features of a particular animal. Pictures from magazines, post cards, and calendars are good visual resources. Many students collect model animals. These models give students a chance to examine animals from different points of view.

Coil animals are a good project for beginners. Encourage students to think of four-legged animals with slim bodies and to describe the animals. How does the animal move? What does the animal eat? What sounds does it make? Consider the specific features and characteristics that make each animal distinctive.

During modeling, students may ask for help with proportion and balance or with arms and legs that come apart. Frustration is short-lived in this activity, because if students dislike their initial results, they can simply ball up the clay and start over.

Objectives

- Distinguish freestanding sculpture from relief sculpture.
- Use the coil method to create freestanding sculptures.

This spunky brown deer by Antoine R.·Hunt, age 8, demonstrates the coil method.

Materials

For each student

- ☐ Clay (1–1¼ pound), soft and well wedged
- ☐ Workboard
- ☐ Pin tool
- ☐ Wood skewer
- ☐ Slip
- ☐ Cardboard tube, 3" (8 cm) in diameter
- ☐ Sponge brush
- ☐ Mini clay extruder (optional)

Clay Alternatives

- ☐ Earthenware clay
- ☐ Stoneware clay
- ☐ Porcelain
- ☐ Raku clay
- ☐ Oven-fired clay
- ☐ Self-hardening clay
- ☐ Polymer clay

Directions

When making a coil animal, allow the body to stiffen a little over the cardboard tube before joining the neck. Occasionally, you may need to dry a moist piece quickly. Heat lamps and hair dryers are convenient for forced drying in this case.

1. Have each student imagine a four-legged animal with a relatively slim body. Good examples include deer, goats, unicorns, lions, dogs, cats, tigers, giraffes, gazelles, and the like.
2. Begin making coils as described in Chapter 4. Remember that to make good coils, the clay should be quite plastic but not wet. Try to keep the coil uniform in thickness.
3. To form the animal's body and legs, roll a large coil, about 1½" (4 cm) in diameter and about 7–8" (18–20 cm) long.
4. With a pin tool, evenly divide the coil lengthwise at both ends. The 2" (5 cm) divided ends form the animal's legs, while the remaining center portion becomes the body. **(A)**
5. Place the split coil on top of the cardboard tube, with the "legs" of the animal dangling over each side. **(B)** Using the tube as a support, position the front and rear legs as desired. Ensure that the legs are strong enough to support the entire figure. Set this assembly aside.
6. To model the animal's head and neck, roll a smaller coil. Bend it to form a "7." Add details appropriate for each animal: eyes, ears, nostrils, mane, or horns. **(C)**
7. Using the pin tool, score the base of the neck where it will join the body. Next, score the body where it will meet the neck.
8. Apply slip to both surfaces.
9. Keeping the cardboard tube support in place, join the neck to the body. **(D)**
10. Make a tail by rolling a small coil or use a mini extruder to make noodle-like clay "hair." Join the tail to the body.
11. Smooth the animal with a damp sponge brush.
12. Remove the mailing tube when the animal is leather hard. Set aside to dry.

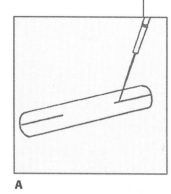

A

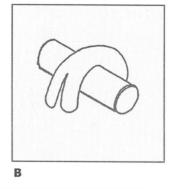

B

C

D

Coil Snake

Young students enjoy making snakes from a single, thick coil. Older students might enjoy decorating snakes by using found objects to imprint designs, or by painting patterns with underglazes. The results are equally attractive.

Coil animal variations by Tim McCord, age 9 (left), and Samantha Verette, age 9 (right). Coil animals stand better if the legs are thick and spread apart.

Coil Sea Monster

Young students love the legend of the Loch Ness Monster. A clay Nessie, swimming through the table, is easy and fun to make.

Roll a long coil about 1" (2 cm) in diameter, and cut it into several 2" (5 cm) sections. Make one short coil into a fearsome or friendly head. Hook the rest of the short coils on the round handle of a large paintbrush (size 12 or larger). Remove the brush when the clay becomes leather hard. Set the sea monster aside to dry.

Students may also experiment with draping a long coil on a row of markers or other similar objects, and making a dragon brush-rest for their art studio.

Dragon brush-rest by Ken Greenleaf, age 11. Ken modeled his dragon using the coil method. He paid close attention to the curves of the dragon body to ensure they could hold several brushes.

Advanced Coil Deer

This piece uses coils of similar thickness except for the details on the head. Note that the legs are far apart for good balance.

Older students are challenged by more complicated coil constructions. An inverted paper food container is an excellent support for drying long-legged animals. Try using them instead of the cardboard tube for coil animals. These containers are made of thin paperboard which adequately supports the clay figures, yet bends easily for removal. Available in a variety of sizes, the containers are tapered in shape, facilitating removal from under shrinking clay.

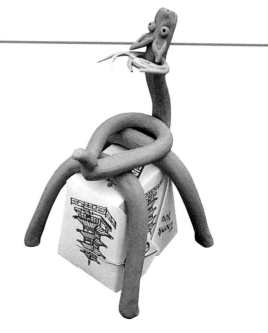

Evaluation Criteria

- Can students make freestanding animals with coils?
- Do students use correct joining techniques?
- Do the clay animals reflect the unique creativity of each student?

Extensions

Interdisciplinary and Multicultural Links

- **Language Arts:** Have students read fables and fairy tales that feature animals.
- **Social Studies:** Research the appearance of animals in sculpture from around the world and throughout history.
- **Science:** Examine how an animal's features are adaptations to its environment and to other animals.

Enrichment Tips

- Take students on a sketching trip to a zoo.
- Provide pictures of animals from magazines and newspapers. These can serve as valuable visual aids.
- Encourage students to make coil animals that belong together such as a doe and a fawn, a stallion and a mare, or a mare and a filly.

7

Animals at Work

Pinch Pot Baskets

Students love to make things that they can use. In this activity, a pinch pot evolves into a basket, and a prancing animal becomes its handle. The best way to introduce this activity is to ask questions such as, "What is the function of a basket?" "What makes baskets different from pots?" and "What do basket designers need to think about?"

Pinch pot baskets provide opportunities to practice previously learned clay skills and to express individuality. Students review basic pinching techniques while making baskets. They learn to roll and apply coils to enlarge and embellish their pots. Adding a creative handle makes each basket distinctive.

Objectives

- Combine learned skills to create a basket.
- Use coils to enlarge the basket form.
- Identify functional objects and sculptural pieces.

A basket with a rabbit handle, Stephanie Callaway, age 9. The rabbit handle is not only decorative, but also functional.

Materials

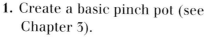

For each student
- [ ] Clay (1½–2 pounds)
- [ ] Slip
- [ ] Brush (to apply slip)
- [ ] Tennis ball
- [ ] An old sock
- [ ] Pin tool
- [ ] Workboard
- [ ] Wood skewer and other found objects for texturing

Clay Alternatives
- [ ] Earthenware clay
- [ ] Stoneware clay
- [ ] Porcelain
- [ ] Raku clay
- [ ] Oven-fired clay
- [ ] Self-hardening clay
- [ ] Polymer clay

Directions

You can enlarge the pot by adding coils. If the pot becomes soft and floppy while you are working on it, let it stiffen a little before adding more coils.

1. Create a basic pinch pot (see Chapter 3).
2. To create the appearance of a woven basket, use a craft stick (or another found object) to imprint a repeated pattern on the pinch pot. This technique is similar to the one used on the turtle shells introduced in Chapter 5.
3. To enlarge the basket, roll several coils that match the thickness of the pinch pot.
4. Measure the length of the first coil against the circumference of the pinch pot. Place the coil on the rim of the pot, and trim the coil ends where they overlap. **(A and B)**
5. Score both ends of the coil with the pin tool, and set it aside.
6. Score across the rim of the pinch pot with the pin tool. Scratch into the clay to make a cross-hatch pattern. **(C)**
7. Brush the rim with slip. Lay the coil on the rim, and press it lightly against the pot.
8. Brush the two ends of the coil with slip to join them together. **(D)**
9. Continue to add coils to the basket, joining each coil to the one beneath by scoring and applying slip. You can control the shape of your pot by placing each coil slightly toward the center or slightly toward the outside. Add coils until the basket is the desired size and shape.
10. For a whimsical basket, create a coil animal (see Chapter 6), such as a rabbit, deer, or snake, for the handle.
11. Attach the handle firmly at the rim of the basket.
12. If needed, place a loose ball of newspaper inside the basket to support the handle while drying.
13. Cover the handle loosely with a piece of wet paper towel; otherwise, the handle may dry faster than the rest of the basket, resulting in shrinkage and cracking.

A

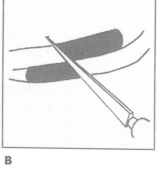

B

C

D

Pinch Pot Baskets

Story Basket

Basket variations by Kyle Frost, age 9 (left), and Abigail Anne Carpenter, age 10 (right).

Older students might enjoy creating a basket that tells a story. The story basket is a twin basket made of two compartments that are joined by an elaborate handle. Select a story, and divide the plot into a beginning, middle, and end. Fairy tales and myths make good subjects. Use the first basket to depict the beginning of the story; decorate the handle to describe the story's middle; use the second compartment to reveal the conclusion of the story.

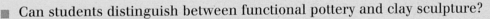

Evaluation Criteria

- Can students distinguish between functional pottery and clay sculpture?
- Can students use coil methods to enlarge a pot?
- Can students combine two modeling methods (pinch pot and coil) to create a new form?

Extensions

Interdisciplinary and Multicultural Links

- **Social Studies:** Explore the relationships between pottery and basket use through Native American history.
- **Language Arts:** Read fantasy literature to inspire related story baskets.

Enrichment Tips

- Compare and contrast functional pottery and sculptural pieces.
- Ask students to bring in cups, mugs, teapots, and baskets. Compare the handles of the various vessels.
- Encourage a discussion by asking the following questions:
  1. How do the handles feel in your hands?
  2. Do the handles complement the form?
  3. Are the handles purely decorative?
  4. Are the handles large enough to hold the weight of the pot plus its contents?
  5. Does the object need a handle or handles?

8

The Watering Hole

Animal Pitchers and Fountains

Objectives

- Construct a water pitcher and understand its function.
- Work in small groups to create water fountains. (advanced students)

Water pitcher in the shape of an animal, Ken Greenleaf, age 11. Ken used red, white, and black underglazes to create a sense of balance.

Handbuilding techniques evolve from simple designs to functional forms. This activity begins with directions for making a water pitcher in the shape of an animal. Then students combine animal pitchers to create a cascading water fountain.

Pitchers can be thought of primarily as teapots without lids. There are many imaginative variations of teapots on display in museums and art galleries. Novelty teapots are available in coffee shops and gift shops. If possible, show students some pitchers and teapots. Discuss the different types and forms.

Among all functional pottery forms, the teapot presents a special challenge for the potter. Most students are familiar with the nursery rhyme, "I'm a little teapot short and stout. Here is my handle, here is my spout." This song points out the important components and characteristics of a traditional teapot. Before modeling the animal pitcher with clay, direct students' attention to the function of a teapot. Show the need to tip it over and pour the tea out. This demonstration helps students understand the relationship between spout position and the water level in a pitcher.

The Eccentric Teapot by Garth Clark contains many pictures of delightful and exotic teapots, and serves as inspiration for this activity. Pictures of gargoyles and carved animal figures may also inspire students.

Materials

For each student
- ☐ Clay (1½–1¾ pounds)
- ☐ Slip
- ☐ Pin tool
- ☐ Tennis ball
- ☐ An old tube sock
- ☐ Workboard
- ☐ A small wood dowel (sharpened like a pencil)
- ☐ Damp sponge brush
- ☐ An old-fashioned butter paddle (optional)

Clay Alternatives
- ☐ Earthenware clay
- ☐ Stoneware clay
- ☐ Porcelain

Directions

To make a crisp twisted rope pattern for the tail, roll your coil across the paddle only once. When piercing the neck tunnel, use a rotating action rather than forcing the wood dowel through the clay.

1. Make a pinch pot using the tennis ball method (Chapter 3).
2. You can enlarge the pinch pot by adding layers of coils (Chapter 7). You can smooth the form by hand or leave the coils showing. The coils themselves provide the piece with inherent design.
3. Enlarge the pot to the desired size, then turn it upside down to rest on its rim. This will become the body of the animal.
4. On the workboard, roll a coil, and cut it into four equal sections. These will become the legs for your animal. Score four areas on the bottom of the pinch pot, where the legs are to be attached. Apply slip to the scored areas. Attach the legs firmly. Work the seams of the legs into the body with the wooden dowel to ensure that the legs adhere to the pot. Allow the pot and the coils to dry to the leather-hard stage. **(A)**
5. Roll a coil for the tail. If you have a butter paddle, you can roll your coil diagonally across the paddle to create a twisted rope pattern. **(B)**
6. Roll a coil slightly larger in diameter than the legs to form the head for your animal. Use the wood dowel to indent facial features. Add ears, horns, or any other details.
7. Turn your animal right side up, so that it stands on its four legs.
8. Score the area where the tail will be

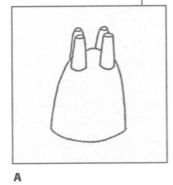

A

B

C

D

attached. Apply slip on the scorings, and attach the tail at the scored point. The tail can be used as the handle of the pitcher.

9. Attach the head in the same manner, scoring both surfaces and applying slip to the joint. To reinforce the joint, place a small clay coil around the base of the animal's neck, and smooth the coil into the seam. This will help strengthen the neck of the animal. **(C)**

10. For the animal pitcher, position the neck so that the mouth is above the anticipated water level in the body.

If the animal is to be used for the fountain project, the neck must be lower than the water level.

11. Support the neck with one hand. Carefully push the sharpened wood dowel into the animal's mouth, creating a tunnel through the neck into the body. Carefully withdraw the tool from the neck. **(D)**

12. Use a damp sponge brush to clean off the debris.

13. Allow to air dry slowly for several days.

14. Fire to maturity and glaze.

Animal Water Fountain

- Large container
- Pebbles
- Battery-operated pump
- Plastic or rubber tubing

Directions

1. You will need two or three animal pitchers to construct a water fountain.

2. Remember to position the neck of your animal as low as possible. When the body is filled with fluid, the water should drain from the animal's mouth by gravity.

3. Place the animals in the large container filled with rocks and pebbles to different heights.

4. Arrange the pots so that when the animal in the highest position is filled with water, the water will drain through its mouth into the next animal. Water should run through each animal until it drains from the lowest animal's mouth into the container.

5. Connect the pump and hose so that the water is drawn from the large container into the topmost animal, establishing circulation.

This water fountain was created from three animal pitchers. The pitchers may be arranged to form a progression. The largest animal may lead to the smaller ones or a resting animal may progress to the animals in motion.

34   **Animal Pitchers and Fountains**

Evaluation Criteria

- Can students explain the relationship between spout position and water level in a pitcher?
- Can students skillfully use pinch and coil techniques?
- Can the animal pitchers hold liquid?
- Do the mouths of the pitchers allow for easy flow of liquids?

Extensions

Interdisciplinary and Multicultural Links

- **Science:** Explore fluid mechanics, including Pascal's law, water cycles, energy sources, electricity, and magnetism.
- **Language Arts:** Research the role of animals as symbols and metaphors in mythology and fables.
- **Social Studies:** Explore the role of water in Middle Eastern, Oriental, and Indian culture. Examine the use of irrigation in the development of agriculture and civilization.
- **Mathematics:** Study volume, density, and units of measure.

Enrichment Tips

- Ask students to name some pots designed for pouring, such as pitcher, decanter, coffeepot, teapot, coffee creamer, and sauce boat.
- Ask students to bring in pots used for pouring, and test how well they work. Does the pot pour without dripping? Does it drip even when it's not being used to pour?
- Find some water fountains and discuss how they work.

9

Egg-Form Creations

Owls

Objectives

- Transform clay balls into simple ovals. (beginners)
- Form imaginative creatures starting with a sphere. (advanced students)

Clay balloon owls by (left to right) Karen Guilkey, Cameron Granger, and Emerich Gutter, all age 10. Each owl has its own distinct personality.

Young students frequently start drawing and modeling in the same manner. Many students begin drawing animals, birds, and fishes with a similar oval shape for the body. Next, they add other shapes to indicate the remaining features. Unguided, young students often start modeling clay by rolling it into balls before pinching or pushing the clay into more definite forms. Making clay balloons will not only advance students' dexterity with clay, but also foster confidence in their abilities. Once students comfortably create the egg form, they will feel capable of modeling any object that they can draw.

This comprehensive activity stimulates ideas, teaches techniques, reinforces manipulating skills, and builds confidence. For young students, start with simple egg-form creations. The following clay owl is a good start for beginners. Older or more experienced students might use the clay eggs as a starting point for their creative adventures.

An important reminder: Do not fire a totally enclosed sphere. The trapped air will expand when heated and will cause the pot to crack or explode during firing. To allow the air to escape, add a pinhole to the sphere before it passes the leather-hard stage.

Materials

For each student
- [ ] Clay (1½–1¾ pounds) well wedged; two balls the size of an orange
- [ ] Slip
- [ ] Workboard
- [ ] Pin tool
- [ ] Craft stick
- [ ] Found objects for texturing tools

Clay Alternatives
- [ ] Earthenware clay
- [ ] Stoneware clay
- [ ] Porcelain
- [ ] Raku clay
- [ ] Oven-fired clay
- [ ] Self-hardening clay
- [ ] Polymer clay

Directions

Reinforcing joints is particularly important when making the owl. The joints are subject to great stress during modeling, texturing, drying, and firing.

1. Begin with two balls of clay about the size of an orange.
2. Create two pinch pots, using the method outlined in Chapter 3.
3. Check the rims of the pinch pots. Ensure that they are even, strong, and have the same circumference.
4. When the pots have dried to a soft-leather stage, score and apply slip to the rims of both pots.
5. Hold a pinch pot in each hand. Join the two pots rim to rim with a slight twisting motion. **(A)**
6. To reinforce the joint, make a small thin coil, and place it on the seam around the joint. **(B)** Work the coil into the clay, and smooth any unevenness with your fingers. The air trapped in the sphere will act as a support, preventing collapse while you add texture and model the facial features.
7. Form eye sockets and a beak by pinching clay between thumb and index finger. **(C)**
8. Add eyeballs and eyelids.
9. Incise the end of a craft stick to make a feathery texture.
10. To form ears, use the pin tool to cut two small "V" shapes on each side of the owl's head above the eye sockets. Pry the triangular ears open, and gently lift them upward.
11. Use the pin tool to cut two large "V" shapes for wings. Pull them open. **(D)**
12. Allow the piece to dry completely, fire, and glaze.

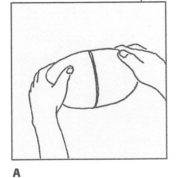

A

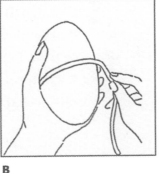

B

C

D

More Egg-Form Creations

Students' imaginations soar as they create dinosaurs and fantastic critters that hatch from these eggs. Using the clay sphere as a body, students can add legs, tails, and other features, using coils or small, rolled-out balls. To make scaly and armor-like skin, provide nuts, bolts, door keys, or discarded, dull saw blades for texture. Encourage students to bring in objects they could use as clay tools for their specific needs. Brainstorming on form and texture opens new avenues for creative expression. Some students may choose to work in groups, initiating their projects with collaborative stories. Each student contributes a figure to a common scene. Others may prefer to create creatures that convey their own individual imaginations.

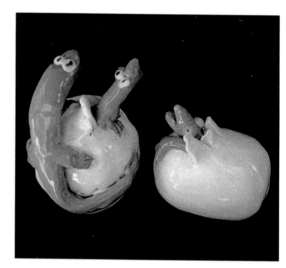

Andrew Abernathy, age 11, made the porcupine body from clay and painted toothpicks to resemble sharp quills.

Above, right:
Fantastic critters hatched from clay eggs were made by (left to right) Kyle Tate, age 11, and Cameron Granger, age 10.

Right:
The imaginary animal and dinosaur hatched from clay eggs. Left to right, Bryan Litton and Alex McCarthy, both age 10.

Evaluation Criteria

- Do students skillfully use pinch techniques to make identical pinch pots?
- Do students correctly join the clay balloons?
- Do students understand why the clay balloons must be pierced before firing?
- Can students transform the clay balls and spheres into personable creatures?

Extensions

Interdisciplinary and Multicultural Links

- **Science:** Research birds, endangered species, and extinct animals. Learn about the role of eggs and eggshells; the diversity of egg sizes, shapes, and colors.
- **Language Arts:** Read or write original stories based on fantastic animals.
- **Art:** Show drawings and other works of art depicting animals made from oval shapes. If possible, display Oaxaca wood carvings from Mexico. Show clay figures of various birds, such as toucans, ducks, and owls, made by people from different cultures. Compare the creations.

Enrichment Tips

- Show pictures of animals and their offspring. Encourage students to make large- and small-scale animal families.
- Encourage students to show how the animals interact.

Part Three

Slab Building

10

Basic Handbuilding Techniques and Glazes

Tropical Fish

- Learn to use the three basic handbuilding techniques.
- Define the terms *greenware, bisque, underglaze,* and *glaze.*
- Describe general safety precautions for glazing.

After developing the pinch and coil techniques of the previous chapters, introduce students to small-scale slab rolling using rolling pins. Students generally find the slab method easy and versatile. It is similar to rolling out cookie dough or pie crust. By joining flat, clay "slabs" rolled to a uniform thickness, students can make geometric forms. Pinching and coiling generally produce round forms. With practice, students can use clay slabs to make almost any form.

Making pots from clay slabs requires novel techniques, tools, and equipment. When slabs are used extensively, a slab roller is essential. However, students should experiment with wooden rolling pins. The goal is to roll the clay to an even thickness throughout the entire slab. You can first cut a large slab from a clay block with the cutting wire. Then practice rolling clay slabs on the workboard with a rolling pin, using two guide sticks to ensure uniform thickness.

Tropical fish supply diverse colors and forms to inspire sculptural creations in art. This clay fish project provides opportunities to use all three basic handbuilding techniques, and offers an introduction to glazes.

William Litton, age 10, threw a clay slab over several large seashells to create the appealing textures on the fins of this tropical fish.

Underglazes are decorating colors used just as their name implies: under a glaze. Underglazes are available in quick, ready-to-use forms. Concentrated, opaque colors are recommended for covering large areas quickly, easily, and smoothly. These colors are useful for detailed painting, sgraffito decoration (produced by scratching through a surface of glaze to reveal another color underneath), watercolor effects, free brush painting, and stamping. Many intense colors are available. Shades and tints are made by blending.

Glaze is a glassy coating used to make clayworks waterproof and decorative. Glazes are classified by appearance (glossy, matte, textured, opaque, translucent, or transparent), color, maturity temperature, and type of firing atmosphere (oxidation or reduction). Many professional potters make their own glazes according to different recipes. When working with students, use the commercially available pre-mixed and lead-free glazes. To ensure a safe and healthy clay program, observe the following important general safety precautions:

- Always choose nontoxic materials, and read all written material about safety precautions.
- Follow application and firing instructions.
- Make sure the work area is well ventilated.
- Clean spills immediately with a wet mop or sponge.
- Before closing jars containing glaze or underglaze, clean the rims with a wet sponge.
- Wash brushes immediately after use.
- Wash hands and arms thoroughly after working.
- Never allow food or drinks in the clay studio.

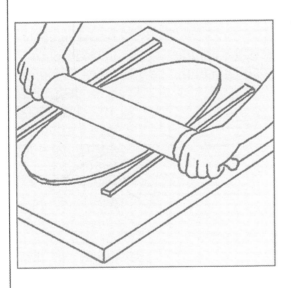

To make a clay slab with a rolling pin, position two parallel wood sticks over the workboard. The wood sticks must be of the same thickness as the slab. Press wedged clay between the wood sticks, and roll it out flush, with the rolling pin riding on top of the sticks.

Materials

For each student

- [ ] Clay (1¾–2¼ pounds)
- [ ] Slip
- [ ] Workboard
- [ ] Seashells and found objects with texture
- [ ] Tennis ball
- [ ] A tube sock
- [ ] Pin tool
- [ ] Hole cutters

Clay Alternatives

- [ ] Earthenware clay
- [ ] Stoneware clay
- [ ] Porcelain
- [ ] Raku clay
- [ ] Oven-fired clay (Use glaze substitutes for surface designs.)
- [ ] Self-hardening clay (Use glaze substitutes for surface designs.)
- [ ] Polymer clay (Use glaze substitutes for surface designs.)

Directions

Raku Fish. A bright yellow underglaze was applied to the middle section of the fish, then covered with a clear glaze, and fired to 1886° F. Raku glazes were applied to the rest of the fish and fired to 1841° F. in a Raku kiln.

1. Make a clay balloon (as described in Chapter 9) for a fish body.
2. Roll out a thin slab of clay about ¼" thick.
3. Press large seashells or found objects on the clay slab to create textures suitable for fish fins.
4. Cut fins in different shapes from the textured clay slab.
5. Roll a small coil for the fish lips and several smaller coils for barbels (slender organs extending from the head of certain fishes) or other facial details.
6. Join the lips, barbels, and fins to the fish body.
7. Allow the fish to dry to the leather hard stage. Cut eyes and a mouth.

Hole-cutters are handy tools for making perfectly round features.

8. Using a pin tool, carefully cut around the gill covers, and pry them open slightly, without disturbing the lip and barbel arrangement.
9. Encourage advanced students to embellish the fish body with small coils. Create additional surface textures by impressing various found objects or by applying thin clay slabs to form a raised design.
10. Allow the piece to dry completely before firing. After bisque firing, dip the bisque into a tub of water for a few seconds before applying underglaze or glaze. The water will displace any loose clay dust that may have collected during firing. Allowing the bisque to absorb some water will produce smoother strokes during painting.
11. Paint the fish with two even coats of underglaze. A spatter brush loaded with underglaze may be used to add interesting texture and shading to the fish. After the underglaze decorations dry thoroughly, apply two thin coats of transparent glaze, and fire to maturity.

Evaluation Criteria

- Do students show proficient use of all three basic handbuilding techniques?
- Have students used correct joining procedures?
- Can students define the following terms: *greenware, bisque, underglaze,* and *glaze?*
- Do students show an understanding of general safety precautions in the clay studio?

Extensions

Interdisciplinary and Multicultural Links

- **Science:** Investigate sea life, coral reef habitats, varieties of tropical fish, and fish adaptations to the environment.
- **Language Arts:** Read fish stories and tall tales. Examine the use of hyperbole in literature.
- **Music:** Listen to sea chants and other work songs.
- **Social Studies:** Locate tropical zones on a world map; identify climate patterns and their influence on cultures.

Enrichment Tip

- Encourage students to read fairy tales and then create clay characters.

11

An Interdisciplinary Unit

Fossils

Objectives

- Use rolling pins to make clay slabs.
- Identify and collect found objects to press into clay fossils.
- Learn to use the slab method to make a clay fossil.

This chapter offers a simple, freeform slab-building lesson and is particularly appropriate in a nature setting. It is suitable for summer camp activities, scout troop projects, or backyard art and science programs. Students can explore outdoors to collect Queen Anne's lace, ferns, leaves, and stalks to press into their fossils. This project also provides an excellent opportunity for students to discover the science of real fossils. Library books can supply valuable historic and scientific information as hands-on clay experience enriches the learning process.

Fossil, Eric Drucker, age 8. This piece demonstrates the possibilities of using watercolors or tempera paints coated with acrylic varnish instead of glaze.

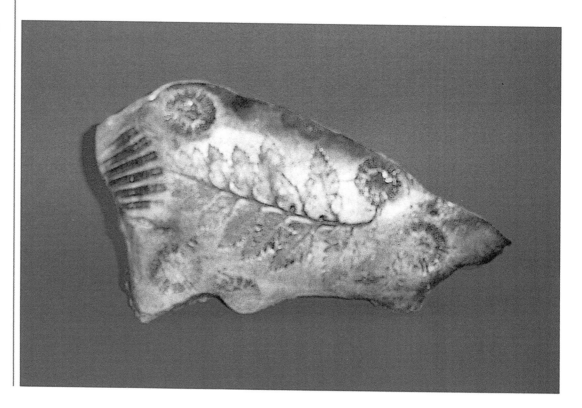

A slab roller is an essential tool for slab building, particularly for large numbers of young students. When you use a slab roller, you can prepare large quantities of clay slabs in advance. Slabs will remain moist for two or three days when tightly covered with plastic sheets. Clay slabs resting under plastic become more pliable and durable. This process is called *seasoning.* Seasoning enhances the workability of the clay by moistening all clay particles in the slabs.

Before working with clay, students should collect "specimens," such as ferns, dill, Queen Anne's lace, bones, shells, or fish skeletons.

Many things in nature make interesting impressions on clay fossils. Use your imagination.

Materials

For each student
- Clay (½–¾ pound)
- Wooden rolling pins
- Workboard
- Pin tool
- Watercolors
- Tempera paints
- Brush
- Elephant ear sponge
- Old newspaper

For the group
- Corn starch
- Found objects

For the studio
- Clear acrylic varnish (available in aerosol spray)
- Slab roller

Clay Alternatives
- Earthenware clay
- Stoneware clay
- Porcelain
- Raku clay
- Oven-fired clay
- Self-hardening clay

Directions

3

1. Roll out an ample supply of ½" (1 cm) thick clay slabs in advance. Cover the slabs with plastic sheets to keep them moist.
2. Tear a piece of clay about the size of your hand from the large clay slab. The irregular torn edges create an interesting natural look.
3. Place the small clay slab on the workboard.
4. Position leaves, stalks, or plant parts on the small clay slab. Press them into the clay by firmly rolling over them with the rolling pin. You may leave plant parts in the clay or gently remove them with the pin tool.
5. Fish skeletons or shells tend to stick to the clay surface. To prevent sticking, dust these objects with cornstarch before pressing them into the clay.
6. Cover a flat surface with newspaper. Place clay fossils on top of the newspaper to dry evenly and slowly.
7. Fire to maturity.

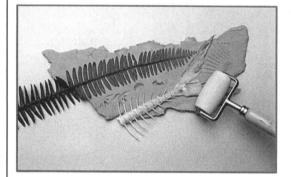

To press delicate objects, use a pastry roller instead of a rolling pin for better control.

Decorations

1. After the bisque clay fossils have cooled thoroughly, dip them in water for a few seconds.
2. Paint the clay fossils with watercolors or tempera paints.
3. After the paint has dried for a few minutes, wipe the higher surfaces of the fossil with a damp elephant ear sponge. This enhances the contrast of the depressions and adds textural interest.
4. Take the clay fossils outdoors or to a well-ventilated area, and apply a coat of clear acrylic varnish to produce a polished appearance.

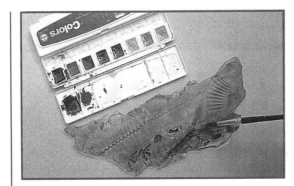
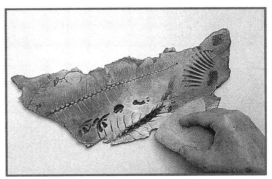

To avoid dry brushstrokes, mix watercolors with a lot of water.

Highlight the depressions in the clay fossil with a damp elephant ear.

Evaluation Criteria

- Can students describe the formation of real fossils?
- Are students able to use the rolling pins to make slabs of even thickness?
- Can students make good impressions in the slabs?
- Can students use watercolors or tempera paints to emphasize depressions?

Extensions

Interdisciplinary and Multicultural Links

- **Science:** Investigate the formation of fossils, prehistoric life, plate tectonics.
- **Language Arts:** Read primary and secondary sources of history; evaluate narrative accounts from different perspectives.
- **Social Studies:** Learn about the development of civilization; discuss time lines and time capsules.

Enrichment Tips

- Take a field trip to a nature museum to view real fossils.
- Write an imaginative story about a fossil hunt.

12

An Easy Slab-Building Lesson for Beginners

Clay Pockets

Objectives

- Use several found objects as texturing tools.
- Learn to use the slab method and proper joining techniques to make a clay pocket. (beginners)
- Learn to combine pinch, coil, and slab methods to make functional and decorative wall planters. (advanced students)

Clay pocket, Catherine Hidalgo, age 10. Catherine created this piece from stamped slabs. The gracefully textured surface enriches the simple form.

A clay pocket is a decorative vase designed to be hung against a wall. Wall pockets have historically been used to hold flowers. The clay pocket design in this chapter features simple construction methods and requires a skill level appropriate for students. The activity emphasizes different techniques for texturing flat clay surfaces. The finished products can function as flower vases, pencil holders, note keepers, or rubber band collectors.

Older and experienced students who wish to expand their clay skills should try the wall planter or the freeform clay pocket.

Materials

For each student
- ☐ Clay (1¼–1¾ pounds)
- ☐ Slip
- ☐ Pin tool
- ☐ Workboard
- ☐ Wood skewer
- ☐ Paper (for making patterns)
- ☐ Pencil
- ☐ Scissors

For the group
- ☐ Slab roller
- ☐ Newspaper

- ☐ Found objects for use as texturing tools (examples: meat tenderizing mallets, rubber brayers, cords, macramé lace, paper doilies, nylon nets, stitchery lace mesh, latchhook rug canvas, ends of markers, seashells)

Clay Alternatives
- ☐ Earthenware clay
- ☐ Stoneware clay
- ☐ Porcelain
- ☐ Raku clay
- ☐ Oven-fired clay (Use glaze substitutes for surface designs.)
- ☐ Self-hardening clay (Use glaze substitutes for surface designs.)

Directions

1. Draw an oval pattern from a piece of paper. The pattern doesn't have to be perfect. Young students can simply trace their hands. Older students may want to design decorative shapes such as hearts, baskets, bears, and so on.
2. Cut out the paper pattern with scissors.
3. Roll out clay slabs about ⅜" (1 cm) thick. If a slab roller is available, slabs may be prepared in advance.
4. Place the paper pattern on top of the clay slab.
5. Following the pattern, cut the slab using the pin tool.
6. Repeat the above two steps to create a second, identical clay slab shaped like the pattern.
7. Place one of the oval clay slabs with its inner side facing up on a flat surface. Set this slab aside.
8. Texture the other oval clay slab. Students may explore the following ways to create texture on clay slabs:

   - Hammer the clay with the meat tenderizing mallet.
   - Wrap cord around a rubber brayer. Roll the modified brayer into the clay slab.
   - With the rolling pin, roll macramé lace, paper doilies, stitchery lace mesh, latchhook rug canvas, or nylon nets onto the clay.
   - Press clay stamps, the ends of markers, rulers, or seashells into the slab.
   - Cut the clay slab into strips, and weave them together using the "over one, under one" plaiting method.
9. Position the clay slab textured side down.
10. With the inner side of both slabs facing up, score around two-thirds of the lower circumference of the clay slabs.
11. Apply slip to the scored areas.
12. Crumple approximately half a sheet of newspaper into a loose patty.

Sandwich the paper patty between the two oval clay slabs. This will hold the interior of the pocket open. Keep the paper patty away from the slab edges.

13. With the textured slab on the top, match the scored areas. Pinch the clay slabs together to form a pocket.

14. Reinforce the seam by pressing the end of a wood skewer along the edges at intervals that contribute to the overall textural interest.

15. Pierce a hole near the top of the untextured slab, so that the finished pocket can be mounted to a wall.

16. You may enlarge the mouth of the clay pocket while the clay is still moist and soft. Peel open the textured clay slab slightly, as if peeling a banana.

17. The newspaper may be left inside. The loose paper patty compresses as the clay dries and will burn off during bisque firing.

Older students can make a wall planter in a similar manner.

1. Prepare a large slab of clay ¾" (2 cm) thick.
2. Texture the surface of the slab.
3. Cut a large oval shape about 10–12" (25–30 cm) long. This will become the back of the wall planter. Set it aside on a flat surface.
4. From the large textured slab, cut a half-oval shape about 4–5" (10–13 cm) long. **(A)**
5. Crumple a sheet of newspaper into a loose ball. Place the small half-oval slab over the newspaper ball. Gently stretch the slab into a slightly convex shape.
6. Return to the large oval slab. Join the half-oval slab, supported by the newspaper ball, to the lower half of the large slab. This is similar to attaching a pocket to a garment. **(B)**
7. Poke a hole 1" (2 cm) from the top of the large slab to permit wall mounting.
8. Further "frame" the wall planter with a few sprays of decorative clay ivy or poke some holes on the lower part of the planter wall to suspend decorative clay bells (see Chapter 23). **(C and D)**

Note: The wall planters, like all large pieces of claywork, need to dry slowly and evenly.

You can make wall planters in many shapes with different decorations. As a rule, the larger the planter, the thicker the slab.

A   B   C   D

Freeform clay pocket. This raku piece is formed by slabs thrown over several large seashells. The piece derives its peaceful, organic character from the shell motif and the irregular silhouette.

A freeform clay pocket is an interesting variation.

1. Cover the floor with a piece of heavy canvas. Arrange a few large seashells or other objects with interesting textures on the canvas.
2. Tear a soft slab of clay like you used to make clay fossils (Chapter 11). Holding the clay slab with both hands, throw it outward and then fling it down on top of the textural objects.
3. This freeform slab will pick up the imprints of the objects on the canvas and hold some interesting patterns.
4. This new clay form can be used as a clay pocket or as embellishment for the wall planter.

Evaluation Criteria

- Can students name several found objects to use as texturing tools?
- Can students make interesting textures on clay surfaces with found objects?
- Can beginning students use the slab method and proper joining procedures to make a clay pocket?
- Can advanced students combine pinch, coil, and slab methods to make a functional and decorative wall planter?

Extensions

Interdisciplinary and Multicultural Links

- **Language Arts:** Explore the theme of gardens and plants in literature.
- **Science:** Learn about seed germination and plant growth.

Enrichment Tips

- Introduce students to art criticism using clayworks as examples.
- Introduce the four steps of art criticism: description, analysis, interpretation, and judgment.
- Lead students in a discussion of the following questions:
  1. What do I see?
  2. How is the work made?
  3. What is the ceramic artist trying to express?
  4. What do I think of the artwork?

13

A Paper and Clay Collaborative Project

Kimonos

Objectives

- Cut a paper pattern for a clay kimono.
- Describe the procedures of using paper patterns for hand-building in clay.
- Create a freestanding kimono.

The kimono is distinctive in its construction and surface design. Kimono construction is based on a simple form sewn along the straight lines of a bolt of material. The straight lines and unbroken surface of the kimono become a pictorial canvas wrapped around a human form. Kimonos are decorated with elaborate designs. All kimonos are the same shape and can be worn by either men or women. In general, men's kimonos have more subdued colors than women's kimonos. Kimonos are worn for everyday events, special ceremonies, and festivals; particularly rare or exquisite forms are sought after by collectors. Over the centuries, the kimono has played an important role in Japanese culture. This versatile garment provides an excellent venue for studying Eastern art and culture.

At this point, students should be confident with their clay-building skills. They should be familiar with the three basic handbuilding techniques, as well as the characteristics of clay in general. Students should be able to join seams that will not crack during drying, and know exactly how wet the clay should be for bending, draping, or positioning. Students continually improve their visual skills by examining the visual elements of their work (line, shape, form, space, and texture).

Kimono with Ginkgo Leaves. This slab-formed raku sculpture suggests a dancing torso. The ginkgo leaves were carefully appliquéd. Artwork from the author's *Dancing Kimono* raku series.

Clay kimonos provide an introduction to freestanding slab construction. For young students, it is helpful to experiment with a three-dimensional kimono built from paper before progressing to clay.

Paper Template

Materials

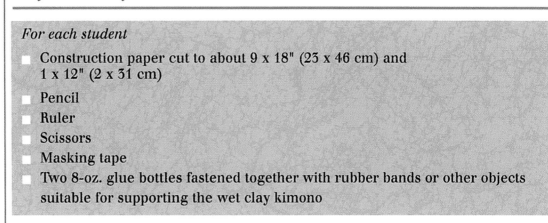

For each student

- Construction paper cut to about 9 x 18" (23 x 46 cm) and 1 x 12" (2 x 31 cm)
- Pencil
- Ruler
- Scissors
- Masking tape
- Two 8-oz. glue bottles fastened together with rubber bands or other objects suitable for supporting the wet clay kimono

Directions

1. Fold the paper (9 x 18"/23 x 46 cm) in half crosswise, then fold it in half again lengthwise. **(A)**
2. With the folds of paper towards the left and the top, use the pencil and ruler to draw a 2 x 6" (5 x 15 cm) rectangle on the lower right-hand corner. **(B)**
3. Grasp the folded edge of the paper, and cut through all four layers of the paper.
4. Unfold the paper, and then fold it again along the central vertical line.
5. Snip off a small triangle to form the neck right below the center cross point. **(C)**
6. Cut open the lower half of the vertical folded line. This will form the front body sections of the kimono.
7. Slightly round the lower corners of the sleeves with scissors.
8. Tape the front body sections to the back section.
9. Supported by two 8-oz. bottles of glue inside, stand the paper kimono upright.
10. Tape a collar strip (1 x 12"/2 x 31 cm) evenly along the neckline and body fronts. **(D)**

A paper kimono template is not only helpful for clay construction, but also can serve as a preliminary design for surface decorations.

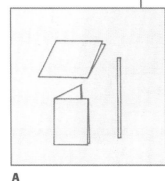

A

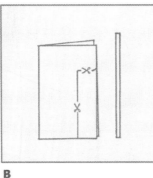

B

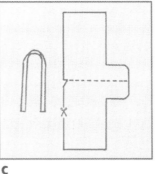

C

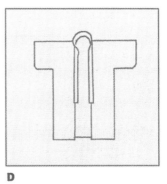

D

Clay Kimono

Materials

For each student

- Clay (2¼–2¾ pounds)
- Workboard
- Slip
- Pin tool
- Ruler
- Sponge brush
- Two glue bottles fastened with rubber bands
- Rolling pin (or slab roller for the group)
- One paper kimono (to use as a pattern), prepared as described previously

Clay Alternatives

- Earthenware clay
- Stoneware clay
- Porcelain
- Raku clay
- Oven-fired clay (Use glaze substitutes for surface designs.)
- Self-hardening clay (Use glaze substitutes for surface designs.)

Directions

1. Roll out a clay slab about ⅜" (1 cm) thick. Let the clay dry to the soft leather-hard stage on a flat surface.
2. On the workboard, place the kimono patterns on the clay slab. Following the patterns, cut the slab with the pin tool.
3. Press the edge of a ruler between the body sections and sleeves to form an armhole seam.
4. On the workboard, drape the kimono over the glue bottles as if putting a poncho over a person.
5. Join the front body sections to the back section. Join the sleeve fronts to the sleeve backs. Pay careful attention to welding the seams together.
6. Roll a thin coil the size of an earthworm, and rub it into each seam.
7. Join the collar strip evenly along the neckline and extend to the body front sections.
8. Smooth all edges of the kimono with a damp sponge brush.
9. Remove the glue bottles when the kimono can support its own weight.
10. Set the kimono aside to dry slowly.

Kimono with Calligraphy, a slab-formed raku sculpture. The bamboo motif represents the essence of morals and the decorative calligraphy depicts "righteousness" in Chinese characters. Artwork from the author's *Dancing Kimono* raku series.

Kimono with Fans, a slab-formed raku sculpture. Colorful fan decorations are created with underglazes before bisque firing. The piece was finished with an even coat of airbrushed raku glaze. Artwork from the author's *Dancing Kimono* raku series.

Students will enjoy decorating their kimonos. They might like to use underglazes or colored slips to decorate their kimonos in Sumi-e style. (This painting style is characterized by simplicity, elegance, and the use of black and white.) Advanced students might appliqué their garments with thin clay slabs in elaborate Eastern motifs. This produces kimonos with a delicate embroidery appearance but requires careful handling during the working process. This is an excellent opportunity to introduce brushwork and to discover Eastern symbols and motifs.

Kimono with Weeping Willow, a slab-formed raku sculpture. The stems and leaves of the weeping willow are arranged as if dancing in a gentle breeze. Artwork from the author's *Dancing Kimono* raku series.

Evaluation Criteria

- Can students explain the differences between shapes and forms?
- Are students able to cut paper templates for clay kimonos?
- Do students use proper techniques to join two clay surfaces?
- Are the finished clay kimonos freestanding?
- Can students evaluate their own work in terms of the visual elements?

Extensions

Interdisciplinary and Multicultural Links

- **Art:** Display and discuss costumes and fabric designs of different cultures.
- **Social Studies:** Use a world map to locate the origin of the displayed costumes. Research the role of climate in determining clothing. Examine traditional versus modern forms of dress; explore changes in clothing patterns and fashions throughout history.

Enrichment Tips

- Discuss the proper clay conditions for bending, draping, and positioning.
- Encourage students to describe, analyze, interpret, and judge their own work.
- Display kimonos or pictures of kimonos, and discuss the use of design elements in Japanese culture.

14

Milk Carton Houses

Show students photographs and illustrations of various kinds of architecture: igloos, adobe dwellings, thatched roof huts, log cabins, modern homes, and commercial buildings. Discuss basic design elements, including line, shape, form, texture, color, and space. During construction, remind students to look at their clay work from every possible perspective. Encourage them to become sensitive to the positive and negative space that they are shaping.

Young students are thrilled with the basic box-shaped house, gable roofs, and simple embellishments. Elementary school students enjoy making their clay houses represent shops in a colonial village. If the roofs are left unattached to the walls, miniature tree lights can be strung from house to house through the removable roofs.

Objectives

- Name different types of architecture.
- Be aware of the purposes of buildings, and distinguish different structures for dwelling, prayer, business, and recreation.
- Make paper templates for their clay houses.
- Make simple box-shaped houses. (beginners)
- Construct more elaborate buildings. (advanced students)

House, Jeffrey Speir, age 10. Southwestern colors and fine detail enhance Jeffrey's image of a California house.

Spirit Houses. Post-fired reduction enhances a crackle raku glaze on these spirit houses. The contrast of black and white colors gives the houses a quiet, secluded feeling.

Older students might enjoy making more elaborate buildings, creating an entire community as a group project. After studying the medieval period through literature and history, middle school students will enjoy making medieval castles. Designing and constructing spirit houses and personal shrines helps stretch creative self-expression and problem-solving abilities for students with advanced clay experience. It is helpful to construct paper models of each design before working with clay.

A clay house may have many joints, which are natural points of stress. It is important to keep the whole piece consistently moist before you begin the drying process. Highly detailed projects such as Victorian homes and reproductions of historical landmarks must progress slowly. Slip mixed with vinegar instead of water keeps the clay from drying too rapidly, and prevents cracking and splitting at the seams. During the drying period, a fine mist of vinegar sprayed over the project helps all parts dry slowly and evenly. Do not be surprised if, after carefully following every step, you still find a crack in one of your pieces. You should be able to repair small cracks in greenware by rubbing vinegar or slip into the cracks.

Materials

For each student
- [ ] Clay (2–2½ pounds) for simple pint-size milk carton house
- [ ] Slip
- [ ] Workboard
- [ ] Pin tool
- [ ] Wood skewer
- [ ] Hole-cutter (optional)
- [ ] Found objects for texturing
- [ ] Paper
- [ ] Tape
- [ ] Pencil
- [ ] Scissors
- [ ] Ruler
- [ ] Paperboard milk carton (pint size)

Clay Alternatives
- [ ] Earthenware clay
- [ ] Stoneware clay
- [ ] Porcelain
- [ ] Raku clay
- [ ] Oven-fired clay (Use glaze substitutes for surface designs.)
- [ ] Self-hardening clay (Use glaze substitutes for surface designs.)

Directions

1. To create the initial design, ask students to make a few sketches of their dream houses on paper. Then have students choose one plan to build in clay.
2. Using the milk carton as a guide, make paper templates for the walls, floor, and roof of the house. Tape the parts together temporarily to approximate the house's size and shape. Younger students might like to wrap a long piece of paper around the milk carton, treating the four walls as one unit. **(A)**
3. Make an ample supply of ⅜" (1 cm) slab available for each student.

For simple houses:

1. Place the four-wall paper template on clay, and cut the clay with the pin tool.
2. Wrap the clay slab around the milk carton. Score the edges and apply slip to join them firmly together. **(B)**
3. Cut a piece of clay to fit the bottom of the house. Join the walls to the floor.
4. When the clay dries to the leather-hard stage, gently remove the milk carton.
5. Fashion the roof with a slab. Some students may like to add chimneys. **(C and D)** Open windows and doors in the same manner as cutting out ears and wings for the owl (see Chapter 9).

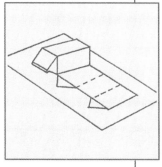

A

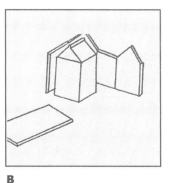

B

C   D

You can paddle the house with a flat ruler or a wooden spatula to define the form and further secure the joints. Be sure to remove the milk carton before allowing the house to dry.

Advanced students may try a more decorative house:

1. On the workboard, place the template on the clay, and cut out all pieces with the pin tool. The clay must be allowed to dry to a soft-leather consistency before any decorative work is done.
2. Cut out windows and doors. Press found objects to texture the walls.

Add shutters, door frames, window boxes, and decorative embellishments while the pieces are flat on the workboard.
3. When clay pieces reach the leather-hard stage, join the walls, floor, and roof.
4. Pay particular attention to all seams.

Evaluation Criteria

- Can students name different types of architecture?
- Can students define the purposes of architecture?
- Are students aware of basic design elements in architecture?
- Can students make paper templates for their clay houses?
- Do students have the basic skills to make a clay house?

Extensions

Interdisciplinary and Multicultural Links

- **Social Studies:** Take a tour of your town or city, and point out different styles of architecture. Research different kinds of architecture, including Egyptian pyramids, Greek and Roman temples, and modern skyscrapers. Discuss the role of cities in the development of civilization.
- **Language Arts:** Draw or make a model of a house, and write a description of the house. Explain where the house is located, describe its various inhabitants over the years, and tell how long they lived in the house and why they left.
- **Art:** Draw, paint, or create collages of cityscapes, dream houses, or a fantastic underground world.

Enrichment Tips

- Show students slides or pictures of different kinds of architecture. Point out details.
- Introduce students to some modern architects, such as Frank Lloyd Wright, Mies Van der Rohe, Le Corbusier, and Antonio Gaudi.
- Visit an architectural firm and learn how architects work.

15

Exploring Pottery Forms and Surface Designs

Flower Vases

From this project, students will learn the concept of two- and three-dimensional representations of an object, and how to incorporate drawing, painting, and marbleizing skills into their clay handbuilding techniques. When students gain a true understanding of the process, they can better articulate their own ideas.

Before you start, show students a wide variety of jars and vases; encourage them to compare shapes, colors, and textures. Divide vase anatomy into five parts that parallel the human body: a mouth (lip), neck, shoulder, belly, and foot. To help students get started, ask them to visualize a person. Surface decoration can be divided into different sections. Use a border design for the lip and foot to frame the main decorative images on the shoulder and belly, or treat the entire piece with a repeated pattern. The predominant consideration is that the surface decoration should not overwhelm the form.

Objectives

- Perceive and identify the basic elements of a vase, and compare vase shapes to the human body.
- Understand the concept of proportion and its importance when creating forms for figures and structures.
- Be familiar with the terms *shape* and *form*, and transform a paper cutout into a clay structure.
- Create a flower vase by combining a flat vase façade and a clay tube.
- Learn to use underglaze or marbleizing techniques to decorate vases.
- Appreciate overall designs that provide continuity and unity.

This glazed flower vase by Bryan Litton, age 9, combines bright colors and strong lines to create a forceful image.

For each student

- [ ] Paper, pencils, and scissors
- [ ] Clay slabs (2–2½ pounds) about ½" (1 cm) thick, rolled in advance with the slab roller
- [ ] Pin tools or fettling knives
- [ ] Cardboard tubes from paper towels or gift-wrap, cut into 12" (30 cm) lengths
- [ ] Slip
- [ ] Workboards or canvas-covered table

Clay Alternatives

- [ ] Earthenware clay
- [ ] Stoneware clay
- [ ] Porcelain
- [ ] Raku clay
- [ ] Oven-fired clay (Use glaze substitutes for surface designs.)
- [ ] Self-hardening clay (Use glaze substitutes for surface designs.)

Creating a Paper Pattern for the Vase Façade

Direction

③

1. Give each student a piece of paper ranging in size from 5 x 8" (13 x 20 cm) to 6 x 10" (15 x 25 cm).
2. Fold the paper in half lengthwise.
3. Starting from the top of the paper, draw horizontal lines from the fold to indicate the width of each part of the vase (mouth, neck, shoulders, belly, and foot). The longer the line, the larger the part. Students must determine whether the neck is to be long or short, the shoulders wide or narrow, the belly large or small, and the foot hefty or small. Encourage individual choices. Then connect the distal ends of these lines with a smooth curve to form the shape of the vase.
4. Cut out the pattern of the vase façade along the pencil line just drawn.

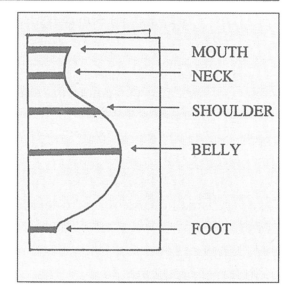

Fold a sheet of paper in half, and draw five horizontal lines to indicate the levels and sizes of the mouth, neck, shoulder, belly, and foot of the vase. Then connect the ends of these lines with a smooth curve to form the shape of the vase.

Making the Vase in Clay

Armed with the paper patterns, the students are ready to work with clay.

1. Unfold the paper, and place the pattern for the vase façade over the clay slab.
2. Cut out the shape carefully by holding the pin tool upright for straight edges.
3. Smooth the edges with moistened fingers, and let the clay vase façade rest on a flat surface.
4. With the pin tool, cut out a rectangular clay slab. The length of the rectangular slab should be about 2" (5 cm) shorter than the height of the vase facade. The width should be 1" (2 cm) longer than the circumference of the cardboard tube.
5. Place the paper tube in the middle of the rectangular clay slab, and wrap the clay around the paper tube as if placing a hot dog in a bun. **(A)**
6. Pinch the extended edges together firmly to make them adhere. **(B)**
7. With the cardboard tube still inside, gently slide the clay tube until the bottom is flush.
8. Lift the entire paper-tube-and-clay assembly, and set it upright on a small piece of clay slab.
9. Cut out a piece of clay to fit the bottom of the clay tube. **(C)**
10. Score both pieces and join them together with slip.
11. Now, return to the resting vase façade. On the flat surface, join the clay tube assembly to the center of the vase façade, making sure their bottoms are even. **(D)**
12. Set the flower vase upright, remove the cardboard tube, and let the vase dry.

Note: Be sure to remove the cardboard tube. If the tube is left inside, the clay will crack as it shrinks upon drying.

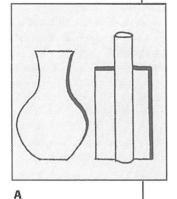

A

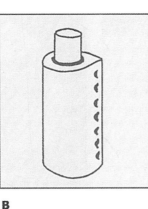

B

C

D

This project works best with "seasoned" clay slabs. Roll out your clay slabs the night before modeling, and cover them with thin plastic sheets. You may find the clay flexible enough to be bent, but stiff enough to stand on its own. If the clay gets dry, mist it with water and let it sit for a while under plastic.

Decoration

After the flower vases are fired, they are ready to be decorated by applying underglazes and clear glaze.

1. Make overall designs that provide continuity and unity to the pots.
2. Draw designs directly on the bisque vases with pencil. The pencil marks will burn off during the firing.
3. Paint the pot with underglazes and glaze. Fire to maturity.

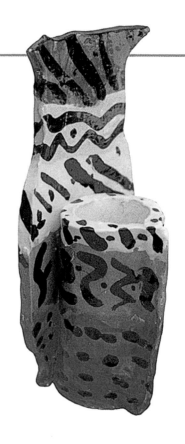

Above:
Bisque flower vases by third grade students.

Above, right:
The back view of Bryan Litton's flower vase.

Right:
Glazed flower vase, Mimi Ballou, age 9. Mimi uses repeated patterns to tie her designs together and create visual unity. Pastel colors and simple designs enhance the elegant shape.

Marbleizing the Vase

Marbleizing is a centuries-old, versatile, and intriguing technique easily applied to clay. Students enjoy experiencing the thrill of instant success.

Marbleizing clay provides an exciting opportunity to experiment with different media.

Materials

- Marbling medium thickener, a nontoxic powder that mixes with warm water to form a thickened solution for floating paints (available from arts and crafts supply stores)
- Droppers
- Marbleizing combs
- Nontoxic acrylic paints
- A sturdy plastic tray twice the size of the vase to be marbleized
- Optional polyurethane glaze

Directions

1. Prepare the marbling solution according to the manufacturer's instructions.
2. Pour the solution into the marbleizing tray.
3. Mix the acrylic paint with water to the consistency of heavy cream.
4. Put a few drops of paint on the surface of the solution. The color should spread out.
5. Dip the comb's teeth at an angle into the surface of the solution, and brush the comb slowly across the tray. Fascinating designs will appear.
6. Grasp the clay tube at the back of the flower vase, and dip the façade into the surface of the solution for 2–3 seconds.
7. The unique design of the solution surface will be transferred to the face of the vase. The bisque vase will absorb the solution instantly. Let the vase dry in an upright position.
8. Repeat the procedure for the back tube, if you wish.
9. When the marbleized images are totally dry, you might apply a coat of polyurethane spray glaze to give the pot a glossy finish.

Marbleized flower vase, Bryce Mueller, age 9.

Evaluation Criteria

- Can students refer to the basic elements of a vase and correctly use terms such as *mouth, neck, shoulder, belly,* and *foot?*
- Do students show an awareness of the proportions of each vase element when making the paper template?
- Do students demonstrate skillful use of the slab method?
- Can students differentiate between shapes and forms?
- Can students create a vase combining a flat vase façade and a tube form?
- Do surface designs appear continuous and united?

Extensions

Interdisciplinary and Multicultural Links

- **Language Arts:** Write a detective story about a priceless vase or an autobiography of a vase. Describe how the vase was made and how it has been used.
- **Mathematics:** Discuss the relationship of volume to surface area. Introduce the ratio of the Golden Mean to middle school students.
- **Social Studies:** Show vases or pictures of vases from different cultures. Lead a discussion of the cultural differences in vase function—storage, decoration, transportation—and proportion. Talk about the influence of a vase's function on its design.
- **Art:** Invite older students to make contour drawings of several vases. For middle school students, set up a still life that includes several different vases.

Enrichment Tips

Guide students to evaluate their own vases by using art criticism skills.

■ **Step One: Description**
1. Show the vase that combines a flat slab and a tube form.
2. Point out the vase that has uniform thickness.
3. Point out the tube form that supports the vase façade.

■ **Step Two: Analysis**
4. Describe the contour of the vase façade using terms such as *mouth, neck, shoulder, belly,* and *foot.*
5. Describe the surface design and explain how to create feelings of continuity and unity.

■ **Step Three: Interpretation**
6. Tell whether the vase is a functional vessel or a purely decorative item.

■ **Step Four: Judgment**
7. Express your own feelings about your work. Tell whether your work is successful and explain why or why not.

16

Facial Expressions

Masks

Objectives

- Perceive and understand the concept of proportion as it applies to the human head and mask making.
- Experiment with cutting and splitting paper collages of facial expressions. (advanced students)
- Create an emotionally expressive clay mask, and select appropriate glazes and other decorative materials to enhance the effect.
- Describe, interpret, and appreciate the design, creativity, and craftsmanship of masks.

Masks have been worn from ancient times to modern day. Primitive tribes wore masks as part of their rituals, festivals, ceremonies, and dances. The masks were thought to give supernatural powers to wearers. Today, masks are found not only in museums, galleries, and gift shops, but also in theaters, carnivals, and political demonstrations. Ask students to bring some masks for "show and tell." Don't be surprised if you end up with a Halloween mask parade!

Below:
Ten masks by fourth grade students. Clockwise from top left: Emily McCracken, Virginia Sanford, Allison Easterlin, Carver Carr, Andy Lane, David Hull, Ben Harris, Peter Elkins-Williams, Steven Suggs, and Eric Drucker.

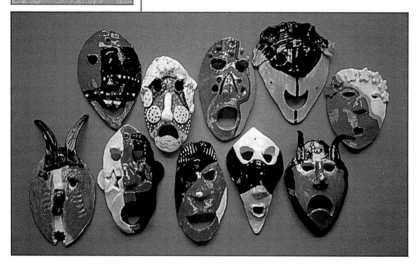

Above:
Mask by Erin Richardson, age 10. Erin creates this strong mystical image using a powerful zigzag line to separate the colors and patterns.

A On a 4 x 6" (10 x 15 cm) dark piece of paper, use pencil to draw a simple face.
B Use pencil to draw horizontal lines to connect each feature to the edge of the paper.
C Cut on the pencil lines with scissors. Arrange all paper cutouts in the same order as the drawing, leaving some space in between.
D Paste all parts on a piece of light paper.

It is likely that many students have made masks from paper bags and paper plates. Most students are fascinated by disguises, pretending, and make-believe. To spark their imagination, display pictures of faces with various expressions. The simple exercise of cutting and splitting paper collages of facial expressions will generate ideas. This experiment is particularly exciting for students because small changes produce radically different expressions. At the same time, the exercise clearly demonstrates positive and negative space. Crisply cut paper lines create powerful, elegant curves. Through the collage exercise, students develop confidence in design and delight in creative expression.

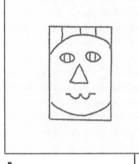

A

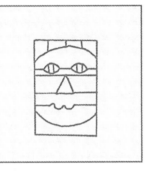

B

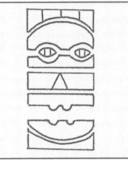

C

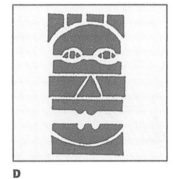

D

Left:
Splitting paper collage, James Friedman, age 10. James uses smooth cutting lines to express anger and strength.

Right:
Splitting paper collage variation, Ben Harris, age 10. Ben combines smooth and intense zigzag lines to express silent rage.

Materials

For each student

- Clay (2–3 pounds)
- Slip
- Pin tool
- Workboard
- Wood skewer
- Newspaper
- Pencil
- Paper
- Scissors
- Round or oval plastic container
- Plaster drape molds (optional)

For the group

- Slab roller

- Cookie cutters
- Found objects for texturing
- Clay extruder
- Butter paddle

Clay Alternatives

- Earthenware clay
- Stoneware clay
- Porcelain
- Raku clay
- Oven-fired clay (Use glaze substitutes for surface designs.)
- Self-hardening clay (Use glaze substitutes for surface designs.)
- Polymer clay (Use glaze substitutes for surface designs.)

Directions

1. On paper, draw the outline of the mask in pencil and cut it out to make a template.
2. On the paper template, write down the emotion that the mask conveys. These will continually remind students of the masks' themes.
3. Distribute an ample supply of clay slabs, ⅜" (1 cm) thick, to each student.
4. Following the paper template, cut the mask from the clay slab with the pin tool.
5. Place the clay mask on the workboard. Fashion the facial features while the mask lies completely flat on the workboard. To decorate the mask, students can exercise the full range of handbuilding techniques.
   - Use cookie cutters to cut out the eyes.
   - Use the owl wing cutting technique (see Chapter 9) for mysterious eyes.
   - Use the clay extruder for instant hair and beards.
   - Interweave coils to make long, realistic braids.
   - Roll a pointed coil of clay diagonally across an old-fashioned butter paddle (from kitchen supply shop) to form a spiral horn.
6. When you are finished modeling, choose a plastic container or a plaster drape mold to maintain the desired curve of the mask.
7. Invert the container, and cover it with newspaper.
8. Drape the clay mask over the container to dry.
9. Remove the mask from the supporting container when it reaches the leather-hard stage. Allow it to dry slowly on a flat surface.

After bisque firing, the masks are ready to be painted with underglazes, followed by a clear transparent glaze.

Remind students to use colors that express the emotion of the mask. Use warm colors such as red, orange, or yellow to express excitement and boldness. Use cool colors such as blue, green, or violet to convey a calm and restful theme.

After glaze firing, students can add raffia, beads, and feathers to their masks.

Encourage older students to evaluate artwork created by their peers. Guide students to make positive comments and to analyze and appreciate the design, creativity, and craftsmanship of others.

Students who want to model small masks might try polymer clay. Marketed as Fimo™, Friendly Clay™, or Sculpey™, polymer clay is versatile, easy to handle, and hardens in a standard kitchen oven. It is nontoxic, has an attractive tactile quality, and comes in many colors. Polymer clay is an

Above:
Mask by Lawson Bradley Williams, age 10. The half-opened eyelids, extended horns, and downward mouth convey devilish spirit. Lawson uses brilliant red, white, and black to highlight the form.

Right:
Mask by Sarah Davidson-Palmer, age 10. The vivid colors and strong textures complement the simple, direct form.

Far right;
Mask by Sarah E. Winstead, age 9. Pastel colors and facial expression enliven this mask. The contour of the piece is soft and expresses the plasticity of wet clay.

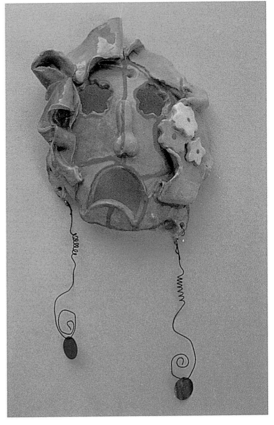

Mask by Rob Bressler, age 10. This mask is strong, fun, and energetic. The lively painted imagery complements and highlights the form.

excellent medium for both school-age students and adults. Although ready-made polymer clay millefiori canes are available, it is easy to create millefiori cane, which is similar to making a jellyroll. Using millefiori cane to create the facial features of the miniature mask will produce an attrac-tive piece of wearable art. There are many polymer clay project books available. *The New Clay* by Nan Roche and the video *Faces, Faces, Faces* by Maureen Carlson are good sources for additional information about polymer clay masks.

Evaluation Criteria

- Do students understand the qualities of lines?
- Can students use lines to express different feelings?
- Do students make facial collages by cutting and splitting paper?
- Are students aware of facial proportions?
- Can students exaggerate facial expressions?
- Do students understand that colors express different moods?
- Do students create emotional, expressive clay masks?
- In critique, can students describe, analyze, interpret, and appreciate the design, creativity, and craftsmanship of each mask?

Extensions

Interdisciplinary and Multicultural Links

- **Social Studies:** Display masks or pictures of masks from around the world. Visit a museum that has a collection of masks, and make sketches from the displays. Learn about the role of masks in different cultures.
- **Language Arts:** Have elementary school students collaborate on a story about a magical mask. Have middle school students write a play that incorporates the use of masks, poetry, dance, and song.
- **Art:** Work with kindergartners and first graders to create paper plate and paper bag masks. Invite older elementary students to make papier-mâché and headband caricature masks. Challenge middle school students to work on self-portrait masks in clay or plaster gauze.

Enrichment Tips

- Suggest that students create a large shoulder mask made of found objects covered with tin foil.
- Invite each student to write a dialogue between his or her mask and one of the other masks.

Cone-shaped Creations

People and Mice

Artists are blessed with the ability to look at everyday things in new ways. Two ordinary bicycle parts—the handlebars and seat—conjoin to form Picasso's *Bull's Head.* Encourage students to look at everyday objects in unusual ways, and to experiment with ordinary objects taken from their usual contexts and brought into new relationships.

These cone-based activities are an outgrowth of these objectives. Conical cardboard yarn spools form the mold for clay cones. Discarded tin cans of different sizes become instant cookie cutters for circular clay slabs. Combinations of clay cones and clay disks produce composite figures, mice, or people. These figures can be assembled as a group project.

Objectives

- **Understand the term** *assemblage.*
- **Learn two ways to create a clay cone.**
- **Use all three basic handbuilding techniques to create a cone-shaped creature.**
- **Experiment with the extruder to add elaborate details.** (advanced students)

Cone-shaped mice by (left to right) Samantha Everette, age 10, Antoine R. Hunt, age 9, Sally Preminger, age 9. Students use all handbuilding techniques to create their forms. Note the way Antoine enlivened the mouse by ruffling its skirt.

Clay Medieval People

Making clay medieval figures is particularly appropriate for middle school students. Encourage students to research medieval costumes, then ask them to make preliminary sketches of medieval figures. Students will enjoy adding details and imaginative props to their medieval figures. Powerful lords, elegant ladies, peaceful monks, and wicked wizards all arise from the earth. Although everyone begins with similar cone forms, no two figures are alike at the end.

A medieval theme lends itself well to this cone-based project.

Materials

For each student
- Clay (2–3 pounds)
- Slip
- Pin tool
- Workboard
- Rolling pin
- Cap from a marker
- Cardboard cone
- Cookie cutters

For the group
- Slab roller
- Extruder

Clay Alternatives
- Earthenware clay
- Stoneware clay
- Porcelain
- Raku clay
- Oven-fired clay (Use glaze substitutes for surface designs.)
- Self-hardening clay (Use glaze substitutes for surface designs.)
- Polymer clay (Use glaze substitutes for surface designs.)

Directions

1. Provide a clay slab ⅜" (1 cm) thick for each student.
2. Wrap the clay slab neatly around the cardboard cone.
3. There are two easy ways to do this:
   A. Cut several clay bands 1–1½" (2–4 cm) in width and long enough to go around the cardboard cone. Start from the lower edge, and gradually work toward the pointed end. Press bands of clay around the cone. Be sure all bands are well joined to form a uniform wall. **(A)**

   B. Cut a large circular clay slab with a radius equal to the height of the cardboard cone. Hold the pointed end of the cardboard cone at the center of this circular clay slab with

A

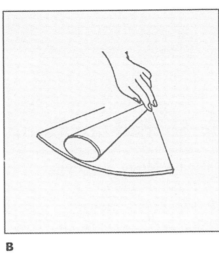

B

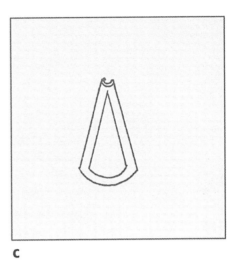

C

Be sure all seams are well joined. Wait until the clay stiffens a bit. Slide your hand into the cardboard cone, and gently remove it with a rotating motion.

one hand, and rotate the cardboard cone along the edge of the clay slab. Mark both the cardboard cone and the clay slab at the start of the rotation. When the cone makes a complete turn, there will be a pie-shaped wedge of clay that will fit the cone perfectly. Cut an inch larger along the edge for a seam allowance. Wrap this slice of the clay slab around the cardboard cone. Trim off the excess clay, and weld the seams together. **(B and C)**

4. To make a hat, use a cookie cutter to cut a clay disk for the brim.

5. Using a cap from a marker, punch a round hole at the center of the clay disk to form a ring.

6. Thread this clay ring over the top of your clay cone. Weld and smooth the seams with fingers.

7. From a small piece of clay, the size of a half-dollar, make a miniature clay mask (see Chapter 16). This will form the face.

8. Join the mask on the cone under the hat where the face should be.

9. Roll a coil about the size of a ballpoint pen. Squeeze and pull to form hands at the ends of the coil.

10. Join the center of the coil to the clay cone where the arms should be.

11. On the workboard, roll out a thin, freeform slab of soft clay. Drape it

over the shoulders of the figure to form a cloak or shawl.

12. For advanced students, select a roughly textured cloth or nylon net, place the textured fabric over the clay slab, and carefully roll out the textural imprints with a rolling pin. Clay cloaks, shawls, or any outer garment made with this method create interesting designs. Be sure to score and use slip to fasten all segments securely.

13. Allow to dry slowly.

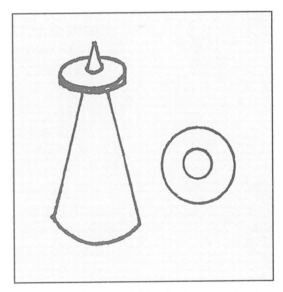

If you want to have a soft fabric look, gently wipe the brim of the hat with a moist sponge and curve it slightly.

More Cone-Shaped Creations

Angels can be fashioned from the same cone form (see Chapter 26.) Mice are favorite characters for young students, and a large wedding party would be an interesting theme for a group project.

Through proper motivation and guidance, students will learn to visualize artistic creations out of simple, everyday objects.

Evaluation Criteria

- Can students make a clay cone?
- Have students joined the seams successfully?
- Are students able to remove the cardboard cones from the clay cone?
- Do students use the three handbuilding techniques to make a cone-shaped creature?
- Are the creatures imaginative and carefully made?

Extensions

Interdisciplinary and Multicultural Links

- **Language Arts:** Write a story about the cone creatures you have made.
- **Mathematics:** Introduce volume and surface area of conical solids. Explore radial symmetry. Use a compass and straight edge to make geometric shapes with circular and polygonal components.
- **Science:** Discuss imagination and observation as important skills in science. Explore radial symmetry in living forms.

Enrichment Tips

- Visit a museum or an artist's studio to learn more about sculpture. Pay close attention to sculptures that include found objects.
- Discuss the importance of assemblage as an art form. Show pictures of assemblages by Joan Miró, Pablo Picasso, and Louise Nevelson. Point out how these artists used their imagination to create unusual art forms from everyday objects.
- Review Chapter 14, and make a cone-shaped birdhouse.
- Review Chapter 8, and make a cone-shaped teapot.

18

A Slab and Coil Combined Critter

Frogs

Objectives

- Use all three basic handbuilding techniques to create fantastic amphibians.
- Work in small groups and establish a unifying theme for their work.
- Hold constructive group discussion and maintain cooperative interaction during the creative process.
- Take responsibility for materials, assembly, and cleanup during each working period.

Some students are dinosaur experts, some are sea turtle specialists, and still others are frog fanatics. It is delightful to watch these students joyfully transform lumps of clay into fantastic amphibians. There are many storybooks filled with wonderful pictures of frogs. These tales can provide inspiration for clay frog projects.

Clay frogs are conducive to small group projects. Through group discussion and cooperative interaction, students can establish a theme for their work. For example, one group of students chose performing arts as a theme, with each frog illustrating a different aspect of music, drama, or dance. The students then formed their own froggy rock band, a green toe ballet company, and a pondside string trio. Each group should be responsible for materials, assembly, and cleanup for each working period. At the end, conduct a critique by encouraging positive comments and suggestions rather than negative remarks.

Pondside string trio, (left to right) Ingrid Smith, age 10, Elizabeth B. Eubanks, age 10, and Greg Bliss, age 10.

Froggy rock band, (left to right) Ritu Mahal, age 9, Alex Kotch age 10, and Molly W. Staton, age 9.

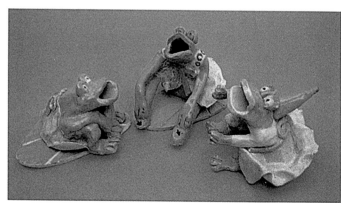

Green toe ballet company, (left to right) Blair Nance, age 9, Catherine M. Clark, age 10, and Lindsay Speir, age 9.

Materials

For each student

- Clay (2–2½ pounds)
- Slip
- Pin tool
- Workboard
- Newspaper
- Wood skewer
- Rolling pin
- Paper, pencil, and scissors (optional)

Clay Alternatives

- Earthenware clay
- Stoneware clay
- Porcelain
- Raku clay
- Oven-fired clay (Use glaze substitutes for surface designs.)
- Self-hardening clay (Use glaze substitutes for surface designs.)
- Polymer clay (Use glaze substitutes for surface designs.)

Directions

1. Make an ample supply of soft clay slabs ⅜" (1 cm) thick for each student.
2. Forming the basic frog body is similar to making a taco (review Chapter 12). Cut an oval slab, slightly larger than one's hand. Beginners may like to make a paper template as a guide.
3. Place the oval slab on the workboard. Score around the edges, except the area for the mouth, and spread slip over the scored area. **(A)**
4. Crumple half a sheet of newspaper into a loose ball.
5. Place the newspaper ball on the center of the oval slab. **(B)**
6. Fold the slab in half like making a taco.
7. Pinch the edges together firmly. Remember to keep paper away from the sealed edges.
8. To make the eyeballs, roll two clay balls, each about the size of a marble. A wood skewer is handy for creating pupils. Attach the eyes to the top of the frog's head. **(C)**

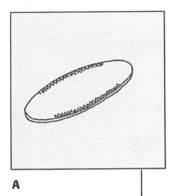

A

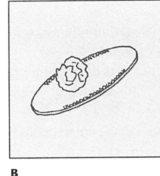

B

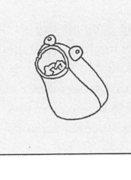

C

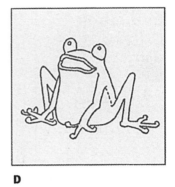

D

You will need soft and well-wedged clay to make this frog. For the details, small pieces of clay crumble easily when handled too much.

9. Roll two long coils. Trim them into two pairs of legs, one pair slightly shorter than the other.
10. Shape the frog's feet by splitting the end of the coil legs into three miniature bananas. Add small beads of clay on each toe for toenails.
11. Join the shorter front legs a bit below the mouth to form the "shoulders."

12. Weld the longer back legs to the side and rear of the frog's body.
13. While clay is still moist, bend the frog legs to the desired position, expressing the intended body language. **(D)**
14. Beginners may simply bend the front leg once, at the elbow area, and bend the back leg into an "S" shape.
15. Allow the frogs to dry slowly.

Decorations

1. After bisque firing, empty the burned newspaper dust from inside the frog. Rinse the bisque frog with water.
2. Apply two coats of underglaze to create interesting designs. Try to decorate the frog using a slip trailer filled with underglazes. The slip trailer is a handy polyethylene squeeze dispenser, similar to a glue bottle.

Underglaze of heavy cream consistency flows through the trail bottle smoothly to create neat strokes in paintings and drawings.
3. When the underglaze designs are thoroughly dry, apply two thin, even coats of clear transparent glaze over the underglaze before glaze firing.

Evaluation Criteria

- Can students use all three basic handbuilding techniques to model frogs?
- Are the frogs well made and expressive?
- Do students offer positive comments during the critique?
- Do students take responsibility for setup and cleanup during each working period?
- Are students supportive, cooperative, creative, and productive?

Extensions

Interdisciplinary and Multicultural Links

- **Language Arts:** Read fairy tales and poems or short stories about frogs. You might consider Mark Twain's *The Celebrated Jumping Frog of Calaveras County* or Beatrix Potter's *The Tale of Jeremy Fisher.* Write original stories about fantastic frogs.
- **Science:** Study frog development, habitat, and anatomy. Contrast amphibians with reptiles. Examine the diversity of different frog species.

Enrichment Tips

- Ask students to collect haiku on frogs, and have them illustrate the images with clay.
- Design functional pottery in the form of frogs, such as frog pitchers, mugs, or vases.

19

A Clay Project with a Statement

Chairs

Visual arts and language arts are natural creative partners. Maintaining written journals during an extensive art project stimulates students to capture, analyze, and preserve their experiences, thoughts, and feelings. The clay chair project provides an excellent opportunity. The journal involves both the mind and the heart, stimulating inner growth during the physical creation of an art form. Journal writing helps students realize that the process of learning and creating is far more important than the final product.

Objectives

- Be familiar with the three basic hand-building techniques.
- Understand that designers plan and model products before full-scale production.
- Assemble a project portfolio including preliminary drawings of the chair from at least two different angles, a paper model of the chair, and a journal recording thoughts and work process.
- Create clay chairs with definite themes.
- Name the chairs or write statements about the clay chairs.

Tree Chair: "Have a seat, and think of your own roots." Sarah M. Wilson, age 10.

Materials

For each student
- [ ] Clay (2–3 pounds)
- [ ] Slip
- [ ] Pin tool
- [ ] Workboard
- [ ] Cookie cutters
- [ ] Found objects for texturing
- [ ] Rolling pin
- [ ] Paper, pencil, tape, and scissors

Clay Alternatives
- [ ] Earthenware clay
- [ ] Stoneware clay
- [ ] Porcelain
- [ ] Raku clay
- [ ] Oven-fired clay (Use glaze substitutes for surface designs.)
- [ ] Self-hardening clay (Use glaze substitutes for surface designs.)
- [ ] Polymer clay (Use glaze substitutes for surface designs.)

Before working with clay, have students make paper models to sharpen their thinking and organizing skills.

Paper Models

Directions

1. Collect pictures of interesting chairs from magazines and newspapers.
2. Discuss the evolution of the chair and furniture styles.
3. Design a dream chair; produce a blueprint of the chair from at least two different perspectives (front and back).
4. Using drawings as guidelines, draw each part of the chair to the exact scale of the final clay chair.
5. Cut out all paper components, and make a paper chair model by taping all parts together.
6. Take time to think through the entire building process. Make a list of the steps for creating the clay chair.

Clay Chair

Directions

1. Make an ample supply of soft and well-wedged clay as well as a seasoned clay slab ⅜" (1 cm) thick for each student.
2. Using basic handbuilding techniques, fashion each part of the chair out of clay, according to the paper model.
3. Use the slip and scoring method to assemble the chair. Pay special attention to joints and seams.
4. Fill grooves and pits with soft clay.
5. Use a damp sponge-brush to smooth out the surface and the edges of the chair.
6. Now the chair is ready for the drying process.

Decorate the bisqued chair with underglazes and glazes. Fire once again. The finished pieces weave together many personal ideas with the pliability and solidity of clay. As a result, these clay chairs possess life, energy, and character.

Winter Chair: "Spring is just around the corner." Elizabeth Stevens, age 9. Pastel color and delicate details enhance this fanciful chair.

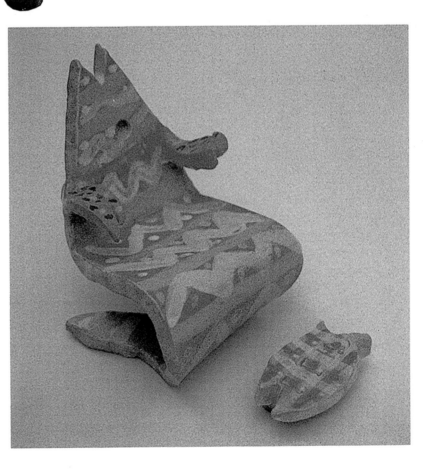

Fish Chair: "I would rather go fishing." Hallie M. Sessoms, age 10. Hallie uses a fish motif for both the lounge chair and footstool. The chair set, reminiscent of a day at the beach, is clever and fun.

Evaluation Criteria

- Are students familiar with the three basic handbuilding techniques?
- Do students make sketches of their chairs from different angles?
- Can students perceive and describe visual elements of the chairs?
- Can each student put together a project portfolio and follow the procedure?
- Do students create a clay chair with a meaningful theme?

Extensions

Interdisciplinary and Multicultural Links

- **Language Arts:** Keep a written journal during the project to capture, analyze, and preserve individual experiences, thoughts, and feelings.
- **Technology:** Write and edit art journals on the computer. Record digital images or drawings of each stage of the clay project.
- **Social Studies:** Collect and display pictures of chairs from different cultures. Discuss furniture style and function in different historical periods.

Enrichment Tips

- Guide students to use art criticism to make aesthetic judgments of the clay chairs. Follow the four steps: description, analysis, interpretation, and judgment.
- Have students discuss how comfortable their clay chairs would be if they were real chairs. Discuss the importance of visual appeal and usefulness to functional objects.
- Invite students to assemble an attractive clay chair display.

Part Four

Clay and Printmaking

Coil Stamp Prints

Rubber Stamps on
Tiles

Relief
Tiles

20

Printmaking through Clay

Coil Stamp Prints

Objectives

- **Understand basic techniques of rolling clay coils.**
- **Make coil stamps.**
- **Predict the appearance of the stamped image from the stamp face.**
- **Press designs into a clay slab, cut out selected sections as stamps, and add strong coil handles. (advanced students)**

Left:
Coil stamp print, David McClay, age 9. David uses a square nail and a chopstick to create strong lines and flowing dots, producing an asymmetrically balanced design for his stamp. He achieves his pattern by alternating the directions of the printing stamp.

Right:
Coil stamp print, Kathryn Leigh Howlett, age 10. Kathryn uses a nail head to make a radial balance motif that forms an intricate floral pattern. The juxtaposition of the prints creates branch-like imagery.

This chapter offers an easy and safe introduction to printmaking. It integrates printmaking and clay through hands-on experiences. A common first exposure to printmaking includes hand and leaf prints in preschool or kindergarten. These early activities introduce the basic elements of printmaking: plate, ink, paper, and pressure.

In early years, teachers often use fruit and vegetable prints to demonstrate repeated pattern designs. However, as a safety precaution, teachers usually cut the vegetable stamps for students. This removes part of the creative opportunity from the printmaking process.

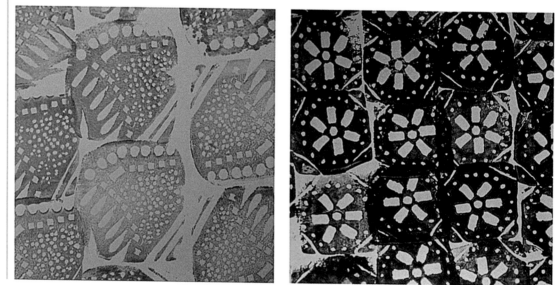

Coil stamp print, Hannah E. Meador, age 10. Hannah uses a small dowel to create a symmetrically balanced design for her stamp. She develops a linear pattern by printing in a regularly repeated fashion.

Making clay stamps restores this aspect to printmaking. Students can make their own stamps safely, creatively, and large enough to fit in their hands comfortably. They can experiment with many creative ways to impress designs into clay.

Materials

For each student
- ☐ Clay (⅛ pound), well wedged and soft
- ☐ Workboard

For each table
- ☐ Cutting wire
- ☐ An assortment of found objects that make interesting stamps (examples: seashells, magic marker caps, hair rollers, earrings, pins, plastic utensils, nails, cord, lollipop sticks, macaroni, wheels from toy vehicles, building blocks, paper clips, nut shells, craft sticks, tree bark, and bottle caps)

Clay Alternatives
- ☐ Earthenware clay
- ☐ Stoneware clay
- ☐ Porcelain
- ☐ Raku clay
- ☐ Oven-fired clay

Directions

1. From a lump of wedged clay, cut off a piece the size of a table tennis ball. Squeeze it into a stubby rope.
2. Place the short clay rope on the workboard and roll it into a fat coil.
3. Repeat these steps to roll several coils about 2" (5 cm) in length and 1" (2 cm) in diameter, one for each stamp.
4. To make the stamp, press interesting found objects directly into the flat end surface of the coil.
5. Combine two familiar objects to create new patterns.
6. Allow the stamps to dry slowly.
7. Fire to maturity.
8. Once fired, clay stamps can be used to add texture to other clay projects.

9. Some more great ideas:

- The soles of athletic shoes make excellent texture tools for coil stamps. Place the shoes on the table, soles up. Locate the most interesting pattern on the sole. Press the clay directly onto the sole to make an impression of the pattern.
- You can make slab stamps by wire-cutting through a block of clay, dividing the slab into small stamp-size clay squares, and pressing interesting objects into the clay surface.
- Another easy way to make clay stamps is to push combustibles that will burn out, such as coffee beans, pasta, or dried pet food, into the clay surface.

Coil stamps made from the bottoms of athletic shoes.

Samples of slab stamps.

Coil Stamp Prints

One hour prior to stamp printing, soak all bisque clay stamps in water. This will prevent the fully saturated clay stamps from absorbing water from the printing inks, and it will produce better inking and printing results. Prepare for printmaking with clay stamps as if printing with potatoes. After using the clay stamps, rinse them thoroughly with clean water. Unlike vegetable stamps, clay stamps can be used over and over again.

Evaluation Criteria

- Can students name several common items that make interesting stamps?
- Can students make simple coil stamps?
- Do students create patterns using combinations of stamps?
- Can students perceive and describe positive and negative spaces?
- Are students familiar with the preparation of bisque clay stamps prior to printing?

Extensions

Interdisciplinary and Multicultural Links

- **Social Studies:** Study the history of the printing press and its role in history. Discover the diversity of the alphabets of various languages. Trace the development of woodcuts to ancient Babylon, Egypt, China, and Japan.
- **Science and Technology:** Explore the typewriter or daisy wheel printer as an extension of printmaking. Visit a local newspaper to observe the modern printing process.
- **Art:** Define the terms *print* and *printing* as used in art. Describe positive and negative spaces. Demonstrate the three steps of printmaking. Explain the use of stamps in Eastern painting.

Enrichment Tips

- Encourage students to use clay stamps in various ways. They might enjoy using the stamps to make gift-wrap or to decorate T-shirts.
- Invite students to create a display about printmaking and clay. Use the display to explain how to make clay stamps and how to use them.

21

Rubber Stamps on Tiles

Objectives

- Perceive and describe the three steps of printmaking: making a printing plate, inking the plate, and printing the image.
- Design a rubber stamp using a sticky foam block.
- Understand the procedures of making flat tiles.
- Use underglazes and rubber stamps to decorate clay tiles.

These slab-formed tiles by Kyle Tate, age 10, and Emerich Gutter, age 9, are decorated with rubber stamps and underglazes.

Decorating clay tiles with rubber stamps further incorporates clay with printmaking. The decorative rubber stamps can serve as both printing blocks and texturing tools for wet clay surfaces.

Major art suppliers stock adhesive-backed foam sheets designed for printmaking. School-age students can draw designs directly on the sheets and cut them out with small scissors. To make rubber stamps ready for inking, students can remove the paper backing from the sheet and stick their designs onto small wood blocks. Local lumberyards or woodworking shops are often willing to contribute scraps. These rubber stamps make wonderful tools for surface design. Young students apply them best to flat surfaces such as tiles or boxes. Using rubber stamps on a curved surface requires the fine motor control of an older student.

For tile projects, particular care should be taken when handling clay slabs during the modeling and drying process. Wallboards are ideal surfaces for working and drying. If you use rolling pins to prepare clay slabs, roll, cut, and dry on the same wallboard. Try to bend or stretch the clay slab as little as possible because clay has "memory." Bent slabs, even after re-flattening, tend to warp during drying or firing. If the slabs are prepared with a slab roller, they will initially rest on canvas. To transport the clay slab to a wallboard, place the wallboard on top of the clay slab, hold the canvas tightly against the edges of the wallboard, and invert the assembly with a swift motion.

Materials

For each student

- Clay (½–1 pound), ½" (1 cm) thick
- Ruler
- Large 90° angles or squares
- Pin tool
- Cutout cardboard squares or rectangular tile templates

Clay Alternatives

- Earthenware clay
- Stoneware clay
- Porcelain
- Raku clay
- Oven-fired clay (Use glaze substitutes for surface designs.)
- Self-hardening clay (Use glaze substitutes for surface designs.)

Directions

1. Roll clay slabs about ½" (1 cm) thick.
2. Place the template on top of the clay slab, and use the pin tool to trace the template's outline onto the slab.
3. Avoid handling the freshly cut clay tiles. Wait until the clay dries to the soft leather stage before proceeding.
4. Cut out a strip of newspaper about 1" (2 cm) wide and 4–5" (10–13 cm) long, and fold it in half lengthwise. Be sure to make a straight crease. Unfold the paper strip, and place the straight, creased line on top of the edges of the tile. Smooth the crease with your thumb and index finger.
5. To produce flat tiles, dry them between layers of wallboards.
6. Arrange all freshly cut tiles evenly on the wallboards with a little space between each tile. Cover tiles with a sheet of newspaper.
7. Continue to stack wallboard on top of each layer of tiles. Repeat this a maximum of two or three times. If the stacks become too tall, the weight will cause the tiles undue stress and restrict shrinkage.
8. Allow the tiles to dry slowly until leather hard. Line them up on a flat surface away from drafts or direct heat sources and continue air drying.
9. Wait until the tiles are bone-dry. Bone-dry clay does not feel cool when placed against the skin.
10. Handle bone-dry greenware very carefully because it is fragile and brittle. Stack the bone-dry tiles flat in the kiln. Put fewer than three layers of tiles on one kiln shelf.
11. Paint the bisque tile evenly with two identical coats of underglaze. This

Use small (sizes 6–8) watercolor brushes to paint underglazes on the cutout designs of the rubber stamps. Be sure to press the painted stamp firmly on the underglaze coated tile.

A

B

will be the background color of the tile. **(A)**

12. Choose another underglaze different from the background color. With a brush, paint this underglaze on the cutout designs of the rubber

stamp. Press the painted stamp on the tile. **(B)**

13. When the underglaze designs are thoroughly dry, apply two even coats of transparent clear glaze over the painted surface.

Evaluation Criteria

- Can students name and explain the three steps of printmaking?
- Can students define *repeated patterns?*
- Are students able to design a rubber stamp using the sticky foam block?
- Can students identify the reversed effect of printing?
- Do students understand how to make flat tiles?
- Can students use underglazes and rubber stamps to decorate clay tiles?

Extensions

Interdisciplinary and Multicultural Links

- **Social Studies:** Assemble a display that demonstrates art as an integral part of life in different cultures. Highlight the use of stamps and tiles. Display fabrics with stamped designs from Africa. Show pictures of tiles that adorn palaces, tombs, mosques, churches, and other public buildings.
- **Language Arts:** Use rubber stamps to create book jacket designs.
- **Art:** Use stamps to create logos or symbols for clubs, special events, and school publications.

Enrichment Tips

- Make inlaid tile trays and mirror frames as individual long-term projects.
- Make inlaid tile tabletops and tile murals as large-group projects.

22

Relief Tiles

Relief tiles have three-dimensional designs on their surfaces. A new, rubber-like material allows for safe, worry-free block printing. Sold under different names at major art suppliers, it can be used to make relief prints and relief tiles from the same block.

This activity is ideal for students age nine and older who enjoy long-term projects. The relief print, relief tile, and printing block make a powerful display.

Objectives

- Be aware of safety precautions while handling lino cutters.
- Make a printing plate by using a rubber-like block.
- Create a relief tile.

A view of a long-term project showing the rubber block, relief print, and relief tile. Classroom demonstrations by the author.

Materials

For each student
- A piece of rubber printmaking block the size of the intended tile
- Lino cutters
- Bench hook
- Drawing paper
- Pencil
- Ruler
- Clay (½ pound)
- Pin tool

For the group
- Printing ink
- Brayer

Clay Alternatives
- Earthenware clay
- Stoneware clay
- Porcelain
- Raku clay
- Oven-fired clay (Use glaze substitutes for surface designs.)
- Self-hardening clay (Use glaze substitutes for surface designs.)

Directions

1. Draw a series of designs about 3" (8 cm) square.
2. Choose a design that will be used for the tile.
3. Transfer the chosen design onto the printing block. The easiest way to do this is to blacken the back of the drawing with pencil. Tape this drawing on top of the printing block. Trace the drawing, and the design will transfer to the block.
4. Proceed to cutting.
5. The technique of cutting is similar to working with linoleum, but the rubber block is softer and easier to cut. A bench hook is still necessary for safety. **(A)**
6. After cutting the entire plate, make a few relief prints on paper to visualize the clay image of the design. **(B)**
7. Older students might explore different compositions by rearranging and juxtaposing the designs.
8. Point out that the textures appearing on paper will be a mirror image

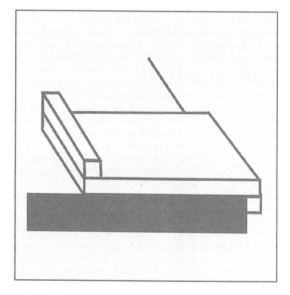

A bench hook rests on the table's edge.

A bench hook is useful for stabilizing the block during cutting. Note the position of the cutting hand in relation to the supporting hand.

A

B

C

of the relief tile. Protuberances on the block will become indentations in the tile.

9. Once the printing block is ready, you can begin to make the relief tile.

10. Roll a clay slab ½"(1 cm) thick.

11. To prevent the tiles from cracking while drying on the wallboard, cover the wallboard with a sheet of newspaper.

12. Press the block on the clay with even pressure. **(C)**

13. Lift the block carefully, and use a ruler and pin tool to cut the relief tile from the slab.

14. Place the freshly cut tile on the wallboard to dry slowly.

Do not press the relief tiles with another wallboard; excess pressure will distort the tile designs. Cover the relief tiles loosely with a thin plastic sheet. Uncover the tiles for five to ten minutes each day. Turn the plastic sheet over each time to free the collected moisture on the sheet. Continue this practice until the tile is completely dry. Carefully controlled and slow drying conditions are required for tiles. Unlike pots, tiles lack the properties that keep a thrown piece in shape as it dries. Many mistakes in handmade tiles prove the truth of Confucius' words: "The desire to have things done quickly prevents their being done thoroughly."

Tiles have many uses, including trays and tabletops. Press a small piece of self-adhesive felt onto the back corners of a tile to turn the tile into a trivet. Young students enjoy the novelty of making fish-tale tile trivets. Simply make a tile shaped like a fish head, and one shaped like a fish tail. Make as many tiles as desired to fit in between. The more body tiles added, the longer the fish grows!

Evaluation Criteria

- Can students describe the three steps of printmaking?
- Do students follow safety precautions while handling lino cutters?
- Are students aware of the reverse effect on prints?
- Can students make printing plates using rubber-like blocks?
- Can students create relief tiles without distorting the designs?
- Do the tiles reflect the students' best efforts?

Extensions

Interdisciplinary and Multicultural Links

- **Science:** Make a collection of leaf prints. Discuss similarities and differences in how artists, botanists, farmers, and archaeologists might look at leaf prints differently.
- **Art:** Review the meaning of relief sculpture. For middle school students, introduce the four main techniques artists use for making prints: relief printing, intaglio, lithography, and screen printing.

Enrichment Tips

- Have students create and assemble a display that focuses on the learning process.
  - Feature the materials used for relief tiles: rubber-like cutting block, lino cutters, bench hook, brayer, and clay slab.
  - Use poster board to write and illustrate step-by-step procedures.
  - Include the printing blocks, relief prints on paper, and relief tiles in the final part of the display.

Part Five

Sound in Clay

Wind Chimes and
Bells

Whistles

23

Melodic Rings and Musical Pinch Pots

Wind Chimes and Bells

Objectives

- Learn to make wind chimes.
- Make a pinch pot with uniform thickness.
- Make a clapper to fit inside the pinch pot.
- Create a bell by attaching the clapper to the pinch pot.

You can make music with clay! Ceramists have made flutes, pipes, drums, trumpets, and sound sculptures out of clay. Strings of clay rings in various sizes mounted on driftwood or tree branches make simple but attractive wind chimes. Students can make wind chimes with very few tools. For this project, you may want to make some cookie cutters from small tin cans. Students can easily poke their fingers through the tops of the cutters to release the clay if it becomes stuck.

Making simple bells is an easy activity for beginners. Once students have learned to make pinch pots, they are ready to make bells.

Four decorative bells, (left to right), Adam Theodore Cloeter Steege, age 9, Laura Solie, age 10, Kathryn Leigh Howlett , age 10, and Krishinda M. Lee, age 10.

Wind Chimes

Materials

For each student
- Clay (1–2 pounds)
- Tin cans in various sizes
- Bottle caps
- Telephone wire

Clay Alternatives
- Earthenware clay
- Stoneware clay
- Porcelain
- Raku clay
- Oven-fired clay (Use glaze substitutes for surface designs.)
- Self-hardening clay (Use glaze substitutes for surface designs.)

Directions

1. Collect bottle caps and tin cans in various sizes, and use an electric can opener to open the bottom of the tin cans. Run the can through the can opener a couple of times to be sure the sharp edges have been pressed down smoothly.
2. Collect telephone wires in multiple colors.
3. Make an ample supply of ½" (1 cm) thick slabs.
4. Cut clay disks of various sizes with tin cans, then press bottle caps or smaller tin cans at the center of the clay disks to make clay rings.
5. Allow the clay rings to dry on a flat surface.
6. After the clay rings are bisque fired, fill several small plastic containers with colored glazes about 1" (2 cm) deep. Students may dip the bisque clay rings into the glazes as if dunking donuts. Attractive freeform patterns will occur between glazed and unglazed areas, as well as where the glazes overlap.
7. Connect the glaze-fired clay rings with various lengths of telephone wire, four or five rings to a strand. Mount a few strings of clay rings to a piece of driftwood. Place them close together so the rings will strike each other when the wind blows.

Bells

Materials

For each student
- [ ] Clay (¾–1 pound)
- [ ] Pin tool
- [ ] Wood skewer
- [ ] Cord, thong, or wire for hanging the bell and attaching the clapper (about 24"/61 cm)

Clay Alternatives
- [ ] Earthenware clay
- [ ] Stoneware clay
- [ ] Porcelain
- [ ] Raku clay
- [ ] Oven-fired clay (Use glaze substitutes for surface designs.)
- [ ] Self-hardening clay (Use glaze substitutes for surface designs.)

Directions

1. To begin, follow the materials list and the directions for pinch pots (see Chapter 3). **(A)**
2. Allow the pinch pot to dry until almost leather hard. Use a hole poker or sharp wood skewer to poke a hole through the top of the pot. **(B)**
3. Make sure the hole is large enough to accommodate a cord or thong.
4. There are two easy ways to make clappers. One is to make a large clay bead that will strike the side of the bell as it moves. A clapper may also be made from a slab that is slightly smaller than the bell. Punch a hole on the top of the clapper with a wood skewer so it can be attached to the bell with a thong, cord, or wire. **(C and D)**

The clay bell will produce a clearer sound if the pinch pot has a thin, even wall and is fired to maturity.

A group of bells may be suspended from a piece of driftwood or other clay work for decoration or as a wind chime.

For a more decorative bell, make a coil animal (see Chapter 6), and attach the animal on the top of the bell like a handle. Suspend the bell by looping a thong around the animal's body. A herd of various sizes will provide fabulous sights and delightful sounds when the wind blows. (See illustration on page 100.)

Carillons are for older students who have acquired basic throwing skills on the potter's wheel. The bells with even, thin walls and flare bottoms are easier to achieve by throwing on the wheel.

A

B

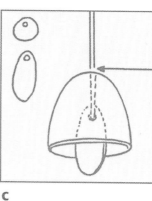

C

D

Bells are thrown like goblets (see Chapter 26). Make a small lug (small handle or ear-like projection) from soft clay, and weld it firmly to the inside bottom of the goblet. The clapper is shaped like a miniature light bulb with a hole at the base. Attach the clapper to the lug with a piece of heavy-duty wire.

Maracas are easy to make with clay. Simply form a clay balloon (see Chapter 9). Before you close the clay ball, enclose a few pea-size clay pellets. Don't forget to poke a pinhole through the clay ball for the heated air to escape.

Raku maracas, made by the author.

Evaluation Criteria

- Can students connect the clay rings to make wind chimes?
- Are the clay ring arrangements visually pleasing?
- Do the wind chimes ring in a light breeze?
- Can students make a bell from a pinch pot with uniform thickness and a properly sized clapper?
- Do the bells ring?

Extensions

Interdisciplinary and Multicultural Links

- **Social Studies:** Discuss the origin of bells. Consider their role in different cultures. In ancient Greece, the ringing of bells signaled that freshly caught fish had arrived at the market. In Rome, bells were used to call people to worship. In the Congo, iron bells were used as a symbol of authority. Using a map or globe, point out the location of famous bells such as the Liberty Bell, Big Ben, and the church bells of Dolores.
- **Science:** Study how the size and thickness of a bell affect its tone. Experiment with "spoon bells" by tying a string to a spoon and holding the string to your ear. Hit the spoon and listen to it ring.
- **Music:** Listen to musical compositions that feature bells or carillons. Demonstrate the technique of playing hand bells.

Enrichment Tips

- Invite older students to add coil animals to the bells as decorative handles.
- Join two pinch pots to create a maraca.
- For advanced students, review Chapter 14, and look at some pictures of Spanish churches for inspiration. Create bell towers with miniature bells.

24

The Sounding Creations

Whistles

It's exciting to make clay sing! Once you have learned to make a clay whistle, you may find it hard to stop. Whistles can be made in many different sizes, designs, and materials. All whistles have a chamber with a sound hole and a mouthpiece with a blowhole. The rule of thumb for a successful clay whistle is to align the blowhole, beveled sound hole, and the connecting air duct properly and neatly.

It is not difficult to make a whistle, but it requires patience. Few tools are needed, and timing is critical. You may want to work on more than one whistle at a time so that you can form one whistle while another is drying. Using the familiar handbuilding techniques in previous chapters, you can experiment with the following ways to make whistles.

Objectives

- Identify the basic elements of a whistle.
- Explain the relationship between the size of the sound chamber and the pitch of the sound that the whistle produces.
- Convert a whistle into an ocarina. (advanced students)
- Transform the whistle into a creature according to the sound it makes.

Bird whistles, (left to right) Lindsay Speir, age 9, and Bryan Litton, age 10.

Materials

For each student
- ☐ Clay
- ☐ Slip
- ☐ Workboard
- ☐ Pin tool
- ☐ Wood skewer
- ☐ Craft stick
- ☐ Rolling pin
- ☐ Plastic Easter egg
- ☐ Small piece of polyethylene food wrap

Clay Alternatives
- ☐ Earthenware clay
- ☐ Stoneware clay
- ☐ Porcelain
- ☐ Raku clay
- ☐ Oven-fired clay (Use glaze substitutes for surface designs.)
- ☐ Self-hardening clay (Use glaze substitutes for surface designs.)

Clay Whistle from One Pinch Pot

Directions

To make the sound chamber:

1. Begin with a small piece of soft clay the size of a golf ball. Make a pinch pot out of this small clay ball. (See Chapter 3. Substitute a plastic Easter egg wrapped with polyethylene for the stockinged tennis ball to help shape the pot.)
2. Roll out a small slab equal to the thickness of the pinch pot wall.
3. Cut a disk of clay from the slab to cap the mouth of the pinch pot. Join the round cap and the pinch pot and weld them together well. Set the pot aside on its cap on a flat surface to dry until the soft leather stage. This forms the sound chamber of the whistle.

To form the mouthpiece:

1. Roll a small coil, about ¾" (2 cm) in diameter and 1" (2 cm) in length.
2. Return to the sound chamber. On the flat surface, join the mouthpiece to the sound chamber like the entrance to an igloo. Make sure all seams are well welded. **(A)**

To cut the sound hole:

1. Be sure the clay has stiffened to the soft leather stage. Hold the whistle with one hand, flat side up.

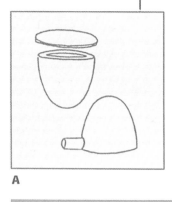

A

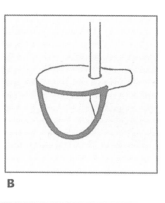

B

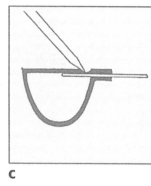

C

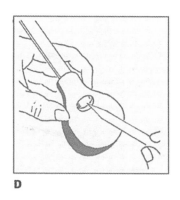

D

Whistle made from one pinch pot.

2. Near the point between the mouthpiece and sound chamber, insert a sharpened wood skewer vertically from the flat top. Direct it into the sound chamber, parallel to the inside wall.
3. Bevel the sound hole by rotating the wood skewer gently but firmly against the edge of the sound hole. The beveled edge should be angled away from the mouthpiece. **(B)**

To form the blowhole and the air duct:
1. Insert a craft stick straight through the mouthpiece beyond the sound hole into the chamber.

2. The craft stick should be visible through the sound hole. Carefully withdraw the craft stick. **(C)**
3. Blow the whistle. Most will sound on the first try. If no sound emerges from the whistle, inspect it for clay crumbs blocking the airflow. Clean, smooth, press, and lift to ensure that all elements are properly aligned. This type of whistle seldom fails. **(D)**

Whistle from Two Pinch Pots

Directions
3

1. Make a clay balloon in an egg shape with two pinch pots. (See Chapter 9. Substitute the polyethylene wrapped plastic egg for the stockinged tennis ball.)

2. Tap the clay balloon gently on a flat surface until one side is flattened a little bit.
3. Proceed to form the mouthpiece, blowhole, and sound hole in a manner similar to the single pinch pot whistle described above.
4. Compared to the single pinch pot whistle, the whistle made from two pinch pots will produce a lower pitch. The smaller the sound chamber, the higher the pitch. For higher pitch thrills, fill the whistle halfway with water and blow.

Bull and cow whistles made from two pinch pots, (left to right) Blair Nance, age 9, and Nadia Wilson, age 9.

Once students are comfortable with the basic form of the whistle, they are ready to make a visual statement. Using the voice of the whistle as inspiration, have them fashion personal creatures. Because whistles are meant to be held and blown, tactile qualities are important. Discourage students from placing long sharp horns or spikes too close to the mouthpiece. Use damp sponge brushes to reduce sharp edges.

There is a standard, widely used method to convert a whistle into an ocarina, a tuned instrument. To make a four-hole ocarina, drill four holes into the sound chamber of a whistle. An eight-note scale can be obtained by covering these holes with the fingers in various combinations. Many elementary school students play recorders, which produce music according to this same principle.

Whistles with inspiring sounds, (left to right) Greg Bliss, age 10, Brendan Walters, age 10, and Julius E. Price, III, age 9.

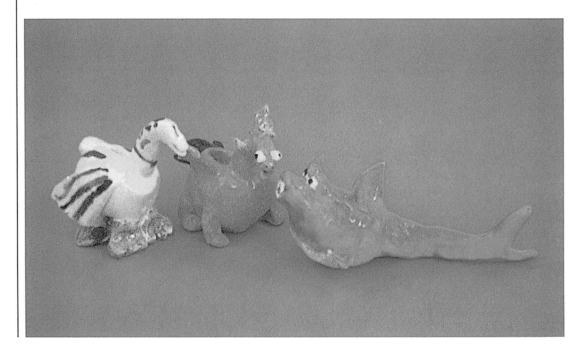

Converting a Whistle into an Ocarina

1. Hold a damp, freshly made whistle with both hands, with the index and middle fingers of each hand on the top, and thumbs underneath.
2. Allow enough room for comfortable fingering. The four fingers mark the corners of a square.
3. To form the ocarina, drill progressively larger holes at each corner of the imaginary square.
4. Use a pin tool to drill the first hole under the right-hand middle finger.
5. The second hole is under the right hand index finger; drill this hole double the size of the first hole.
6. Drill the third hole double the size of the second hole, and under the left middle finger.
7. The fourth hole is under the left index finger and twice as large as the third hole.

Tuning an ocarina is too difficult for elementary age students. Freestyle tweeters can bring as much joy to those young hearts.

Evaluation
Criteria

- Can students perceive and describe the basic elements of a whistle?
- Do students understand that whistles can be made with one or two pinch pots?
- Are students aware of the relationship between the size of the sound chamber and the pitch of the sound that the whistle produces?
- Can each student create a whistle?
- Do the whistles have good tactile qualities?
- Do students demonstrate patience and significant effort?
- Are students able to decorate the whistle depicting the unique sound that it makes?

Extensions

Interdisciplinary and Multicultural Links

- **Social Studies:** Discuss the use of whistles in daily life by police officers, ships, trains, and sports officials. Identify the origins of whistles and ocarinas. Have students find out what *ocarina* means in Italian. *(small goose)*
- **Science and Technology:** Learn how air travels through a whistle. Investigate air compression and expansion, and discover how sound waves are made. Explore the mechanisms of whistles, horns, klaxons, and sirens. Discuss the difference between music and noise.
- **Music:** Show samples of ocarinas or pictures of ocarinas from different countries. Introduce students to recorders.

Enrichment Tips

- Make more musical instruments out of clay.
- Make a clay drum by stretching a piece of leather over a large pinch pot.
- Make a tall drum by stretching a piece of leather over two or three pinch pots that are joined together in a tall stack. Remind students to cut off the bottoms of the top and middle pots. Weld all seams carefully.
- Make clay flutes out of hollow clay tubes.

Part Six

Large Group Projects

A Chess Set

Dinnerware

25

Neptune Charges Forth

A Chess Set

Objectives

- Select themes through brainstorming.
- Make at least one part of the chess set.
- Promote comradeship and collaborative learning.

Large group clay projects add a dramatic element to the creative process. Students learn many valuable lessons through comradeship and shared aesthetic experiences. Each student is responsible for a vital component of the project. In the end, everyone experiences the satisfaction of a greater accomplishment.

Group projects require extensive preparation and careful organization. Project themes emerge best when students brainstorm. For example, sea turtle studies spawned chess sets with a sea creature theme. By blending mythological legends and biological facts, students married King Neptune to a mermaid queen. They molded dolphins as stately bishops. Graceful sea horses became knights, and sandcastles grew into rooks. Sea turtle pawns led the charge.

Creative thinking is the key to success. Once students decide on a theme, allow them to imagine that the clay project is a play. Each student creates a character. Together, students select the color scheme for the sets. Two colors, one light and one dark, are needed. Although the sea chess sets shown in this chapter were made by a group of nine-year-old students, this activity is also suitable as a long-term individual project.

Chess set group project by twenty-two third grade students. Courtesy Dr. and Mrs. Richard S. Stack.

Materials

For each student

- [ ] Clay (½ pound)
- [ ] Slip
- [ ] Pin tool
- [ ] Wood skewer
- [ ] Rolling pin
- [ ] An empty thread spool (2"/5 cm in height, 1¼"/3 cm in diameter)
- [ ] Underglazes and glazes
- [ ] Brushes

Clay Alternatives

- [ ] Earthenware clay
- [ ] Stoneware clay
- [ ] Porcelain
- [ ] Raku clay
- [ ] Oven-fired clay (Use glaze substitutes for surface designs.)
- [ ] Self-hardening clay (Use glaze substitutes for surface designs.)
- [ ] Polymer clay (Use glaze substitutes for surface designs.)

Directions

The clay pedestal resembles an empty thread spool.

The pedestal:

1. Using a rolling pin, prepare a small slab of clay ⅜" (1 cm) thick.
2. Cut two clay disks 1¼" (3 cm) in diameter. **(A)**

3. Roll a small coil 1⅜" (3 cm) long and ½" (1 cm) in diameter. **(B)**
4. Join a disk to each end of the small coil. **(C)**
5. Now you have a clay pedestal. **(D)**

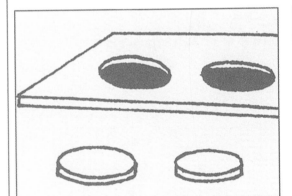

A

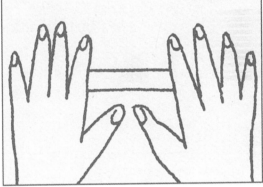

B

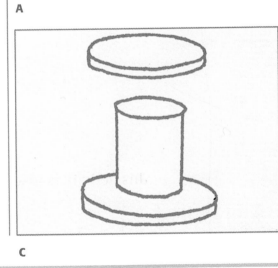

C

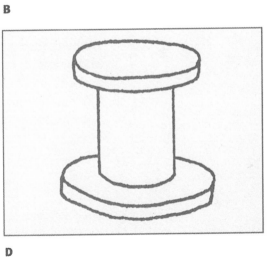

D

The chess piece:

1. Use basic handbuilding techniques to model a small character for the chess piece. **(A)**
2. Refer to the pedestal for proportion and balance.
3. Join the small character to the pedestal. **(B)**
4. Set aside and let it dry slowly.

5. Bisque fire the greenwares when they are bone-dry.
6. Decorate the bisques with under-glazes and glazes.
7. Students should work in groups, monitoring each other's creations for proportion, variety, color harmony, and visual unity.

Be sure the character sits well on the pedestal. If it is too big, it might tip over.

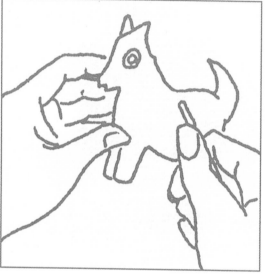

A

B

The chessboard:

1. Make sixty-four 2"/5 cm-square tiles out of a clay slab. If you can find a pastry cutter of the right size from a kitchen shop, that will be a big help. Otherwise, a ruler and pin tool will work.
2. You can also buy commercial tiles from building suppliers.

To make the chessboard, use a pin tool and ruler to cut tiles from a soft, leather-hard clay slab.

3. To complete the chessboard, you will need thirty-two dark tiles and thirty-two light ones, according to the selected color scheme.
4. Glue the tiles onto plywood backing or to a wooden box top.

To complete the chessboard, apply adhesive to the plywood and position the tiles.

Evaluation Criteria

- Do students select appropriate themes?
- Can students handle a multistage project?
- Do students work collaboratively?
- Does every student participate?

Extensions

Interdisciplinary and Multicultural Links

- **Science:** Research endangered species, preservation of tropical rain forests, and promotion of human rights.
- **Language Arts:** Explore fairy tales, nursery rhymes, and mythology.

Enrichment Tips

- Make a chess set with jungle animals as a theme. You might include a lion king, a giraffe queen, antelope knights, monkey bishops, elephant rooks, and toucan pawns.
- Show cookbooks with inspiring color pictures of food. Make a clay banquet with assorted delicacies for all to feast their eyes on.
- Visit a farmers' market or flea market. Afterwards, students can create a clay marketplace.

26

Serving Up the Masters

Dinnerware

Objectives

- Learn about several famous master artists.
- Decide on decorative motifs and dinnerware color schemes.
- Promote comradeship and collaborative learning.
- Decorate dinner plates with stamped designs combined with line drawings. (younger students)
- Apply underglaze to the goblets with rhythmic lines and mixed stamped patterns. (older students)
- Make place card holders and napkin rings. (older students)
- Make salad or dessert bowls using the draping method, and make candlesticks as center pieces for the dinnerware collections using all three handbuilding techniques. (advanced students)

Building 396 pieces of dinnerware is an enormous undertaking for any potter. At Durham Academy in North Carolina, 264 students have done just that! The students who were fortunate enough to have this incredible experience all agreed it was a cinch.

When you attempt a large group project, keep in mind that work distribution is crucial. The number of students should match the number of tasks. Age and skill level are the main factors for determining individual assignments. Overly difficult tasks detract from the fun and interest of the project.

This project addresses the key disciplines of art education—art history, art criticism, aesthetics, and art making—by combining clay and graphics in an age- and skill-appropriate manner.

Dinnerware: Monet Collection, grades 1-4. Photograph by Jim Thornton, *Durham Herald-Sun.*

The students at Durham Academy selected four favorite artists and studied the style of each one. Next, the older students did research. Then they submitted color scheme and decorative motif proposals. After extensive brainstorming, students decided the Picasso sets should feature the sophisticated dove and cubism designs in black and white. *Water Lilies* inspired the color and motif for the sets patterned after Monet. Matisse's *Jazz* series played an important role in the dinner set designs. Blue, pink, white, and purple were chosen as the expressive colors

for the angel motifs. The earth tones of green, brown, and yellow dominate the Rousseau collection. Various animals and plants reflected Rousseau's imaginary jungle.

Each place setting includes a dinner plate, goblet, salad or dessert bowl, place card holder, napkin ring, and a set of candlesticks. The students made two sets of eight place settings for each of three artists (Picasso, Monet, and Matisse). Three sets of six place settings were fashioned in the style of Rousseau.

Dinnerware: Picasso Collection, grades 1-4. Photograph by Jim Thornton, *Durham Herald-Sun.*

Dinnerware: Matisse Collection, grades 1-4.
Photograph by Jim Thornton, *Durham Herald-Sun.*

Dinner Plates

1. First graders decorated the dinner plates with underglazes.
2. Students used stamps and trail bottle-drawn lines to embellish the dinner plates.

3. Students applied two coats of transparent clear glaze to each plate. Particular attention was paid to the glaze application on pieces that will hold food or drink.

Goblets

1. Second graders applied underglazes to the goblets with stamps, brushes, and trail bottles. Students used rhythmic lines, freehand animals, and mixed stamped patterns to adorn the goblets.

2. Students applied two coats of transparent clear glaze to the cups before glaze firing.
3. To finish the goblets, students glued wooden pedestals painted with lead-free enamel to the clay components.

Place Card Holders

Third graders made the place card holders and napkin rings. Before students work with clay, fasten several pieces of 8' long, 1 x 4" (2 x 10 cm) wood strips between sturdy wood stools with the 1" (2 cm) edge upright.

1. Provide an ample supply of ⅜" (1 cm) thick clay slabs.
2. To make place card holders, cut individual 4 x 6" (10 x 15 cm) slabs with the pin tool.

3. Using cookie cutters, cut small slabs in the shape of water lilies, animals, doves, or angels, or make them freeform. Join them near the short ends of the small rectangular slab.
4. Gently fold the small slab in half endwise, and hang the slab on the 1 x 4" (2 x 10 cm) wood strip to dry until leather hard.
5. Remove from the wood strip and continue to dry upright on a flat surface.

Dinnerware: Rousseau Collection, grades 1-4.
Photograph by Jim Thornton, *Durham Herald-Sun.*

Napkin Rings

1. Collect cardboard paper towel tubes, one for each student.
2. Provide an ample supply of ¼" thick clay slabs and well-wedged soft clay for each student.
3. To make a napkin ring, roll thin coils the size of a pencil. Make a ring around the paper tube with either one single coil or twist two thinner coils together.
4. Use vegetable cutters or cookie cutters to cut water lilies, animals, doves, or angels. Join the clay cookie to the ring.
5. Let the napkin ring dry slowly.

Salad or Dessert Bowls

Salad or dessert bowls were made using the draping method. All sets start with a basic oval or round template about 8" (20 cm) in diameter.

1. Each group working on the same set of dinnerware should allow for minor modifications from one piece to another.
2. Working in groups, cut paper templates for bowls.
3. Make an ample supply of ⅜" (1 cm) thick clay slabs available.
4. Place the template on top of the slab, and trace the outline with a pin tool. Smooth the edges with a damp sponge brush.
5. Drape the bowl on a plaster mold or a plastic container, in a manner similar to forming the masks (see Chapter 16).

Candlesticks

Using all three basic handbuilding techniques, fourth graders made candlesticks. They brainstormed for a way to connect all the candlesticks to make a candelabrum. At the same time, each candlestick had to separate for easy handling during construction and firing. Never underestimate students' creativity. A brilliant idea came from a fourth grader. She suggested cutting uniform slab rings, like a large pizza with a small pizza cut out from the center (see Chapter 23). This clay ring could be divided into four equal sections. Each student could attach a candlestick to one of these slab wedges. The base slab not only defined the size of each candlestick, but also served as a connection between each piece. When four candlesticks faced each other, an attractive circular candelabrum appeared. When the candlesticks were placed next to each other, a line of graceful curly lights enchanted the diners.

To make the candlesticks for the Monet collection:

1. Cut two small round clay slabs, 3" (8 cm) and 5" (13 cm) in diameter.
2. Cut notches around the edges to resemble flower petals.

Clay Alternatives
- Earthenware clay
- Stoneware clay
- Porcelain

3. Join the two round flowers on the base with the smaller flower on top of the large one.
4. Make a clay ring to fit a candle, and join it to the center of the flower.
5. The finished image represents pink and white water lilies floating on a light green pad.

Students made a candlestick shaped like a white dove for the Picasso collection.

1. As in making a clay turtle (see Chapter 5), begin with a pinch pot as a body.
2. Roll a coil to form the head.
3. Cut slabs for wings and a tail.
4. Join a clay ring that fits a candle to the center of the pinch pot body.

Cone-shaped creations (see Chapter 17) came alive in the form of angels. A blue and white angel holds the candle illuminating Matisse's dream of "an art of balance, of purity, and serenity." Coil animals (see Chapter 6) make their appearance in the center of Rousseau's table. Striped tigers, long-necked giraffes, and galloping horses celebrate the artist's imagination.

Evaluation Criteria

- Can students identify the artists' styles?
- Can students choose decorative motifs and color schemes after researching their artists?
- Did students hold group conferences to share ideas and evaluate progress?
- Can students perceive and describe repeated patterns?
- Are students aware of the relationship between lines and shapes while decorating the goblets?
- Are place holders and napkin rings of good tactile quality?
- Are salad and dessert bowls well made? Are the edges smooth?
- Do the candlesticks keep the candles upright?
- Do students demonstrate their ability to work independently and cooperatively?

Extensions

Interdisciplinary and Multicultural Links

- **Art History:** Display works of art by Picasso, Monet, Matisse, and Rousseau. Encourage students to read about the lives and work of these artists. Discuss similarities and differences in these artists' work.
- **Language Arts:** Use works of art as writing topics. Have students describe and analyze selected works of art. Through careful observation and group discussion, nurture aesthetic judgment and art evaluation.
- **Art:** Draw, paint, or make collages after the styles of the chosen artists.

Enrichment Tips:

- Create a tea set in the style of your favorite artist.
- Encourage students to practice the four stages of art criticism. Discuss the importance of art history, art criticism, aesthetics, and art making in a quality clay program.

Health and Safety

Labels

Clay, glazes, studio equipment, and pottery-related products are available from many reputable art supply companies. As required by federal law, labels that conform to ASTM D-4236 provide the most accurate and consumer-oriented information on potentially dangerous art supplies. Users may also request a Material Safety Data Sheet (OSHA form 20) from the manufacturer.

The Art and Creative Materials Institute, Inc. (ACMI) administers a voluntary testing and labeling program that helps to ensure the safety of those who work with art materials. This system uses the labels CP, AP, and HL. Products bearing the CP Certified Products Seal and the AP Approved Product Seal are evaluated as nontoxic. Products bearing the HL (Health Label) are either nontoxic without warnings or bear appropriate hazardous ingredient labeling and require instructions. Any products with warnings are required by law to be used only by students in grades seven or higher or by adults who can read and understand the label.

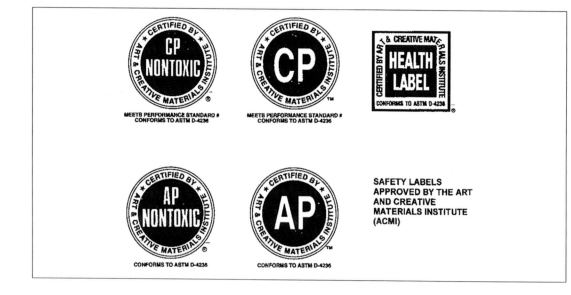

SAFETY LABELS APPROVED BY THE ART AND CREATIVE MATERIALS INSTITUTE (ACMI)

Clay

Clays contain silicates and varying amounts of crystalline-free silica. Inhalation of silica dust from handling clay in dry form can lead to silicosis or "potter's rot." The Center for Safety in the Arts (5 Beekman Street, Suite 1030, New York, NY 10038) recommends use of only wet, remixed, talc-free clays at elementary and secondary schools. Use CP/AP lead-free, pre-mixed liquid glazes only. Total Shop CleanAir System, Industrial Dust Collectors, or Smoke Buster air cleaners are designed to collect airborne dusts created by mixing dry clay or sanding greenware.

Clay Storage

Large quantities, up to 500 pounds, of ready-to-use, moist clay are best stored in airtight plastic bags stacked in a heavy-duty, rustproof, high-density, polyethylene storage cart. Smaller (20 gallon) clay containers with tight-fitting lids and a dolly are suitable for regular classroom use. Major art suppliers carry these products.

Clay Equipment

A slab roller is an essential tool for production handbuilding. Many different models are available. Vinyl backed canvas, available from Axner Pottery Supply Company, eliminates wrinkles in clay slabs.

Plaster is a material of great value to the potter, who uses it to make bats and molds of various kinds. Drape molds are widely used in schools. AMACO drape molds come in seven different shapes and sizes. Drape clay slabs over these molds to make bowls, platters, masks, and dishes.

Kilns

The use of a kiln for firing ceramics is safe if a few common sense precautions are taken.

• Be sure that your kiln is properly installed and that installation meets all local electrical codes. Check individual kiln installation instructions to be sure that your kiln is the required distance from the wall. This distance may vary from 12" to 18" (30 x 46 cm) depending on the type of kiln.

• Kilns—both electric and fuel-fired—should be vented.

• If possible, the kiln should be kept in a separate room to avoid excess heat in the work areas. This also helps to prevent accidents if children are present.

• Wear dark-shaded glasses (shade number 1.7–3.0) for looking into the peephole and protective kiln gloves when handling a hot kiln.

• Only a qualified adult should operate or touch a kiln.

Aerosol Sprays and Solvents

Health and safety experts agree that aerosol sprays and solvents are among the more dangerous art materials, if not used properly. All aerosol spray fixatives should be used only in well-ventilated areas. Avoid breathing vapor, dust, or mist. Use a window exhaust fan or spray booth to remove vapors and assure cross ventilation. Refer to the label for specific information. Solvents should also be used only in a well-ventilated area away from any type of heat or fire.

Common sense and good housekeeping rules should always be followed. Children and pregnant women should not use these materials. When spraying oil or solvent base products, use extreme caution. Wear protective gloves. Use these products only in a well-ventilated area, away from heat or open flames. Use a spray booth equipped with an explosion-proof motor and a strong fan exhausted to the outside. Wear a NIOSH-approved respirator for organic vapors. Always follow OSHA's guidelines for use of products containing solvents.

Spraying and Airbrushing

The technique of airbrushing underglazes and glazes onto greenware or bisque is common in ceramics, and is often taught to high school and college level ceramics students. Safe and proper rules for airbrushing must be taught and enforced in any classroom or studio.

Airbrushing should be done in an exhaust-ventilated spray booth specifically designed for this purpose. NIOSH-approved dust masks should also be worn for safety. Airbrushing is an exciting ceramic decorating technique and need not be avoided if proper safety precautions are used. *Glazes containing lead should not be airbrushed; there are suitable lead-free glazes for this purpose.* Airbrushing for pre-school and elementary age children is not recommended. In high schools, airbrushing should only be introduced under strict supervision.

Glossary

Air bubbles: Pockets of air in clay. These are worked out of damp clay by wedging.

Alumina: The only oxide of aluminum; an ingredient of clay and of feldspar. It is refractory, and therefore raises firing temperatures of ware.

Assemblage: Three-dimensional work of art consisting of many different pieces assembled together.

Asymmetrical balance: Unlike objects have equal visual weight.

Banding wheel: Round turntable used in handbuilding and in applying glazes.

Bisque: A clay object that has been shaped, air dried, cleaned, and fired at an appropriate temperature (determined by the type of clay used) to produce a strong durable piece ready for decorating. Clay cannot be moistened and reconditioned for reuse after a bisque firing.

Bisque firing: A preliminary firing of unglazed ware. While bisque firing temperatures may vary widely, the most common are cones 08–06. The bisque fire prepares the work for glaze application; the ware can be immersed in the watery glaze without cracking or breaking down.

Body: The clay material from which a pot is made or the pot itself.

Bone-dry: Thoroughly dry. Clay that is bone-dry will not feel cool and is very light in comparison to moist or leather-hard clay. Used to describe greenware.

Centering: Adjusting clay so that it rests in exact center of the potter's wheel head for throwing.

Ceramics: A word of Greek origin *(keramos)* that means *burned earth.* Ceramics include not only pottery, but any article made of clay, in whole or in part, that has been heated (fired) to harden the clay.

Clay: A natural product of the weathering and decomposition of rocks, comprising the minerals aluminum oxide, silica, water, plus impurities. Clay is plastic when wet and permanently hard when fired. See also PLASTIC CLAY.

Clay body: One of a number of mixtures of natural clays and other ingredients. The resulting substance will react in predictable ways to certain processes, and will have special properties that any natural clay alone might not possess.

Coil: A rope-like roll of clay used in handbuilding.

Coiling: A means of building up a clay pot or vessel from coils or ropes of clay that are joined together in the plastic stage.

Combing: Sometimes called *feathering*, a process whereby slip is trailed on wet clay, then a fork, comb, or feather is dragged through the wet slip to create a ripple pattern.

Cones: Test cones for temperature indicators are made with various fluxes to bend at given temperatures in kilns.

Crackle: Deliberate crackle lines induced in a glaze for decoration.

Dipping: A method of applying glaze to biscuit-fired ware. Slip can also be applied to greenware by dipping.

Distortion: The twisting of raw shapes that are dried too rapidly.

Earthenware: Pottery that is usually soft, opaque, and porous without a glaze. Good earthenware should become watertight when glazed at a higher temperature.

Elements: High-resistance wire coils made from an alloy used as the heat source in an electric kiln.

Elephant ear: A natural sponge for smoothing and cleaning greenware.

Engobe: A layer of liquid clay or slip that is applied to clay surface as a coating. It may be painted on with a brush, sprayed on, poured on, dribbled on, or dabbled on with a sponge. The layer of engobe may fall off unless the clay of the piece and the engobe shrink at the same rate and in the same amount.

Extruder: A tool into which moist clay is loaded and then pushed through a shaped opening in the end to produce blocks, strings, or ropes of clay. Small extruders, such as a garlic press, are often used by the home craftsperson.

Feathering: A feather tip or brush dragged across wet slip for decoration or for marbleizing.

Fettling knife: A handy tool for removing mold mark, carving clay models, and general clay work.

Firing: Applying sufficient heat for the necessary length of time to promote chemical change and eliminate all water from clay or glaze, thereby causing permanent hardening. *Bisque firing* makes air-dried greenware more durable and easier to decorate. *Glaze firing* causes chemical changes in glazes and other finishes on bisqueware and bonds them to the ware. Temperature and time required for firing depend upon the type of clay or glaze used and conditions in the kiln.

Foot: A supporting rim on the bottom of a clay vessel.

Glaze: A formulation of finely ground glass, suspended in a liquid with the aid of gums, used to decorate the surface of clay objects. Glaze melts when fired and bonds to the clay surface in a colored or clear glasslike coating. May be glossy, eggshell, matte, textured, etc., depending upon formulation.

Glaze firing: A cycle during which glaze materials are heated sufficiently to melt and form a glassy coating when cooled.

Granite: A rock that contains quartz, mica, and feldspar. When the rock decomposes, its feldspar becomes clay.

Greenware: Air-dried, but unfired, clay objects that have been shaped by casting slip, hand modeling, or throwing on a potter's wheel. Although it holds its shape and is dry to the touch, it is still raw clay and is fragile until fired.

Grog: Finely ground, fired clay added to clay body to reduce shrinkage and plasticity or to impart texture.

Impressing: A method of decorating by stamping into a clay surface.

Inlay: A process in which clays of more than one color are worked together to create a multicolored effect.

Kiln: A type of oven in which clay objects are fired.

Kiln furniture: Shelves, stilts, props, and so on, that are used to support pottery when it is packed in a kiln.

Kneading: The mixing of plastic clay by hand (and in some countries by foot) to a good consistency for throwing or modeling.

Lead: A metallic element once used extensively as a flux in glazes and in low and medium temperature glazes; because of its poisonous properties, lead is no longer used in factories and seldom in studios in its raw state.

Leather hard: Clay that is only partly dry; damp enough to cut with a knife and to handle without losing its shape.

Lug: A knob, ear, or projection used on the sides of pottery as a handle.

Marbled ware: A method of using slip on wet ware. If colored slips are allowed to run, they produce a marbled appearance.

Matt glaze: A dull surface obtained by a deliberate mix of the glaze.

Maturing temperature: When clay or glaze achieves desired characteristics.

Maturity: When applied to clay bodies, *maturity* refers to an optimum point at which warping and brittleness are kept to a minimum and the absorption rate is reasonably low. When applied to glazes, *maturity* is the point at which the glaze produces a desired effect. Generally, glazes are *mature* when they are fully melted in the fire and glassy.

Mishima: Decorative technique in which slip is applied over textured clay and then scraped away when dry, leaving slip in the depressions.

Mold: A plaster or bisque clay shape from which a clay form can be reproduced.

Non-fired finishes or stains: Decorative colors (clear or opaque) that are applied to bisque pieces and require no further firing. *Any object to be used as a container or server for food should have a fired glaze finish with a lead-free glaze.*

Overglaze: Decorative technique; color applied to an already glazed and fired piece is fused through low-temperature firing; also a colorant.

Overglazes: Decorative finishes such as metallics, lusters, china paints, etc., that are applied over a fired glaze finish.

Oxidation firing: A firing in which there is ready access of oxygen to the firing chamber at all times. Electric kilns in general are constructed in such a way as to fire in oxidation.

Paddling: Beating clay with a flat stick to strengthen joints, thin walls, alter shape, create texture.

Peephole: An opening in the kiln wall that allows the crafter to inspect the interior of the kiln chamber during firing.

Plastic clay: A ready-to-use, premixed clay in moist form with special ingredients that keep it from hardening so it can be reused; also, a moist clay that is particularly pliable and desirable for hand modeling.

Plasticity: The quality in clay that renders it easy to shape.

Porcelain: Compounded clay that is white, translucent, and very hard and glassy when fired.

Porosity: The capacity of a clay body to absorb moisture.

Pottery: Clay shapes that have been fired to 932° F. (500° C.) or more and have become another substance when the water of plasticity is driven off.

Pyrometer: An instrument that registers the heat within the kiln.

Radial balance: Type of balance in which forces or elements branch out from a central point in a circular pattern.

Raku: Japanese firing process. In this country, it involves the rapid firing of ware, removed hot from kiln and reduced by covering with combustible material.

Reduction: During firing, the oxygen is reduced by cutting down the air flow. This produces a smoky, reduced atmosphere in a fuel kiln.

Reduction firing: Firing with a minimum amount of oxygen. In reduction firing, the potter interrupts the flow of oxygen to the firing chamber of the kiln at certain crucial periods during the firing. This is most naturally accomplished in the fuel-burning kiln. Reduction firing strongly influences the character of clay bodies and glazes.

Rib: A tool used on the outside of pots during throwing.

Sgraffito: Decorative technique; a design is scratched through one or more layers of slip or glaze, producing patterns from contrast between layers or between slip and clay.

Shrinkage: The process of a clay piece becoming smaller as a result of water evaporation during air drying or chemical changes during firing. This normally ranges from ten to twenty-five percent, depending on the type of clay.

Silica: A crystalline material that, along with alumina, is one of the building blocks of all clays and glazes.

Slab roller: A machine that produces slabs of clay. It consists of two rollers—one fixed, the other movable—between which the clay is passed.

Slip: A mixture of clay and water used to hold clay pieces together, or a mixture of clay (or clays) and water with some non-clay materials, that is applied to the surface of a clay piece for decorative effect.

Slip trailing: The use of a squeeze bottle or syringe to apply engobe to the clay to create a raised pattern.

Stain: Single coloring oxide or oxides in combination with other materials used as a colorant or as decoration.

Stamp: A hard column of clay or plaster with a raised pattern on one end used to impress patterns in moist clay.

Stoneware: High-firing clays, hard and vitrified when fired; color ranges from light tans to darker greys.

Sumi-e style: A type of painting that forms one of the great traditions of Eastern art. Sumi-e style is distinguished by its simplicity, lucidity, elegance, and use of black and white.

Symmetrical balance: Type of formal balance in which two halves or sides of a design are identical.

Template: A cardboard cutout used as a guide for shaping the walls of a clay piece.

Texture: The *feel* of a piece of pottery. A smooth surface, a sandy surface, a combed surface, and so on, will give a certain appearance to a pot and a distinctive feel when touched.

Throwing: The making of shapes on a potter's wheel.

Trailing: Slip decoration trailed from a squeezed bag or plastic bottle onto raw pottery.

Underglaze: In ceramics, opaque or transparent colors used on greenware or bisque before pieces are glazed.

Warping: Clayware losing its shape (curling, twisting, distorting) due to improper drying and/or firing. Uneven walls in hand-shaped pieces may cause trouble unless carefully dried.

Wedging: Cutting and de-airing clay before throwing.

Welding: A technique for joining two clay surfaces. Both surfaces are scored, moistened with slip, and pressed firmly together. The seam is then carefully smoothed.

Bibliography

Berensohn, Paulus. *Finding One's Way with Clay.* New York: Simon and Schuster, 1972.

Chapman, Laura H. *Discover Art.* Worcester, MA: Davis Publications, Inc., 1987.

Clark, Garth. *The Eccentric Teapot.* New York: Abbeville Press, 1989.

Gaitskell, Charles D., Al Hurwitz, and Michael Day. *Children and Their Art.* New York: Harcourt Brace Jovanovich, Inc., 1982.

Gatto, Joseph, Albert W. Porter, and Jack Selleck. *Exploring Visual Design.* Worcester, MA: Davis Publications, Inc., 1987.

Gibson, John. *Contemporary Pottery Decoration.* Radnor, PA: Chilton Book Company, 1987.

Gilbert, Rita and William McCarter. *Living with Art.* New York: Alfred A. Knopf, Inc., 1985.

Giorgini, Frank. *Handmade Tiles.* Asheville, NC: Lark Books, 1994.

Hobbs, Jack and Richard Salome. *The Visual Experience.* Worcester, MA: Davis Publications, Inc., 1991.

Hopper, Robin. *Functional Pottery.* Radnor, PA: Chilton Book Company, 1986.

Lambert, David. *The Field Guide to Geology.* New York: Facts On File, Inc., 1988.

Lane, Peter. *Studio Ceramics.* Radnor, PA: Chilton Book Company, 1983.

Moniot, Janet. *Clay Whistles.* Plainfield, NH: The Whistle Press, 1989.

Nelson, Glenn C. *Ceramics: A Potter's Handbook.* New York: Holt, Rinehart and Winston, Inc., 1971.

Nigrosh, Leon I. *Claywork.* Worcester, MA: Davis Publications, Inc., 1986.

Peipenburg, Robert. *Raku Pottery.* New York: The Macmillan Company, 1972.

Peterson, Susan. *The Craft and Art of Clay.* Second Edition, Woodstock, NY: The Overlook Press, 1996.

Ragans, Rosalind. *Arttalk.* Mission Hills, CA: Glencoe Publishing Company, 1988.

Ragans, Rosalind and Jane Rhoades. *Understanding Art.* Mission Hills, CA: Glencoe Publishing Company, 1992.

Rhodes, Daniel. *Pottery Form.* Radnor, PA: Chilton Book Company, 1976.

Robinson, Delia. "Whistle-Stop in Grenada." *Ceramics Monthly,* November 1993, pp. 90–95.

Roche, Nan. *The New Clay: Techniques and Approaches to Jewelry Making,* Rockville, MD: Flower Valley Press, 1992.

Rossol, Monona. *The Artist's Complete Health and Safety Guide.* New York: All Worth Press, 1994.

Sakade, Florence. *Origami: Japanese Paper-Folding.* Rutland, VT: Charles E. Tuttle Company, Inc., 1959.

Topal, Cathy W. *Children, Clay, and Sculpture.* Worcester, MA: Davis Publications, Inc., 1983.

Trevor, Henry. *Pottery Step-By-Step.* New York: Watson-Guptill Publications, 1966.

Trimble, Stephen. *Talking with the Clay.* Santa Fe, NM: School of American Research Press, 1987.

Triplett, Kathy. *Handbuilt Ceramics.* Asheville, NC: Lark Books, 1997.

Wachowiak, Frank. *Emphasis Art.* New York: Thomas Y. Crowell Company, Inc., 1977.

Zakin, Richard. *Electric Kiln Ceramics: A Guide to Clays and Glazes.* Second Edition, Radnor, PA: Chilton Book Company, 1994.

Zakin, Richard. *Hand-Formed Ceramics.* Radnor, PA: Chilton Book Company, 1995.

Index